Prayer Weapons 2015

A Prayer Devotional For You

Emmanuel .O. Olowokere

Prayer Weapons 2015
Copyright © 2014 by Pray Network Inc.

All rights reserved. No part of this book may be reproduced or transmitted in any form or by any means without written permission from the author.

All Scripture quotations are taken from the King James Version of the Bible.

ISBN 978-0-9914852-2-2

Published in USA by Pray Network Inc.

Dedication

This 2015 Prayer Devotional is dedicated to God Almighty, the One that is able to do exceeding abundantly above all that we ask or think, according to the power that works in us. The only God who answers prayers and to whom all flesh come.

Mary Lond
August 1, 2015

Table of Contents

Introduction 5
Chapter 1 9
Chapter 2 37
Chapter 3 55
Chapter 4 73
Chapter 5 89
Chapter 6 105
Chapter 7 125
Chapter 8 139
Chapter 9 155
Chapter 10 169
Chapter 11 183
Chapter 12 205
Epilogue 225

Introduction

What a privilege and honor again to introduce to you the 2015 prayer devotional book and the prayer weapon of 2015. Without any doubt this is a year that God has determined to bring a difference into the life of His people. And the instrument of prayer is one of the avenues, which God's people can align or connect with God's determination.

In Jeremiah 29:11, after God expressed His concern and desire of the future of His people saying, *the thoughts that I think towards you are thoughts of peace and not of evil to give you a future*. Verse 12 says, *and then shall ye pray*. Every determination of God must have a prayer response. That is why it is important for every believer to know that whenever God tells you something you have a promise. The promise must provoke in you the desire to pray. This 2015 prayer devotional will help you not just to pray, it will also give you appropriate scriptures to use and most importantly will give you faith to hope for an answer from Heaven.

This devotional is made up of several sections for each month. It starts with a brief teaching designed to charge you up and inform you about the word based prayers for that month. Prayers follow this. Prayers for you to pray are written in bolded fonts. Finally, there is a teaching for the month designed to build up your faith as you pray concerning that month.

The teachings are prophetically spoken into your life to charge you up and get you in the right frame for the subsequent prayers. In addition, this book is a companion to the Prayer Weapons for 2015 CD series.

I want you to understand that these prayer topics are relevant to you not just in 2015 but also beyond. There is no miracle you are praying for in 2015 that does not apply to 2016. My counsel to you are as follows: you can plan to pray all those prayers throughout the month for the month for e.g., throughout the month of January, you may decide to just pray the prayers for January.

Alternatively, you can decide to dedicate 12 days to praying for the year so that you can address a month per day. If you add fasting to it, it'll make your prayer very effective; Fasting does not make God bigger nor make your prayer stronger but it makes you to be more receptive to receive. Fasting increases your spiritual capacity to take more from GOD and makes your prayers effective. Jesus said in

Mark 9 verse 29 *And he said unto them, this kind can come forth by nothing, but by prayer and fasting.*

On the other hand, you may decide to use every beginning of the month, the 1st day of the month to pray for that month. However you choose to use it or are led to use it, and as the Holy Ghost helps you, just make sure you pray those prayers and you will come back with results by HIS Grace.

As you use this material, I believe that God will transform your prayer life. Your prayer life will become changed, become more exciting and you will find love and joy for prayer in the name of Jesus.

I am glad that God gave us the privilege to make this book ready for you, for your family, and for our generation. It is going to be a blessing and I believe that the testimony God will give you will be heard all over the world in the name of Jesus Christ.

It is a joy to share this material with you as God has put it in our hands. I congratulate you ahead of your testimony, as I trust that God Almighty will do wonderful things for you.

Thank you for getting a copy or several copies. Thank you for using it because the more people who get committed to using it, the more prayer-minded people and intercessors we can raise, for our generation that desperately needs prayer.

God bless you and give you a prayer altar that hell cannot break down. Remain lifted and experience maximum from now and for the rest of your life.

God bless you in Jesus name. Amen.

Chapter One
January 2015

My Brethren, I welcome you into the arena of the Ancient of Days. Where you find His presence on His Holy Hill, where His presence releases us into fullness of joy.

You are also welcome into the first month of the year and our beginning journey into 2015, our Year of Maximum under this prophetic order.

Without a doubt God's thought for us has not changed. He said in Jeremiah 29:11, the thoughts I think toward you, are thoughts of peace and not of evil, to give you an expected end. Your heart should be secured and glad, because His thoughts towards you are thoughts of peace and not of evil. So ahead of you are great and wonderful things.

Fearful praise commands fearful wonders. Moses said in Exodus 15:11 *Who is like unto thee O Lord among the gods? Who is like thee, glorious in holiness, fearful in praises, doing wonders*?" Fearful means you praise Him in such a way that people will say you must be praising a mighty Lord. You give God such praise that angels will consider you a competitor. That is giving God fearful praise. After fearful praise, God's ability to do wonders becomes activated.

It's glorious to know that your praise can win you a place with God. To have a place in the land of the living, your praise must be secured.

My Father, I am here today to offer you my praise, to offer you my thanksgiving, to offer you adoration for preserving me to see today and for all you have done.

For the blessing of preservation, I thank you. Father, be glorified, be magnified, be exalted for preserving me from the 1st day of January till today.

We know that thanksgiving is a responsibility and assignment of the living. The living must praise Him. It's not optional. When it comes to praise, it is mandatory for the living. From scriptures we know everyone is a potential victim, if God does not allow you to escape. The Bible says in Psalm 124:6, *Blessed be the Lord, who hath not given us a prey to their teeth.* If God did not allow you to escape you would have become a prey.

Many have become prey by air disasters, road disasters and suicide disasters, but you escaped 2014. Lift up your two hands, and say:

Father, I thank you for allowing me to escape in the year 2014.

I was reading a report, that in the air space of America there are drones. These drones are intended to monitor the activities on the ground, however on four occasions last year, some commercial jets almost collided with the drones. You don't know whether the airplane you were in was among the ones that almost collided with the drones. If your plane collides with a drone, the results would be catastrophic unless God delivers you. So, even when you think things are safe, you are not really safe. It's simply because God has allowed you to escape.

After I read that report, I began to put drones under subjection, because God forbid if one dies by drones, the family will only receive apologies. In 2014, almost three hundred people left Amsterdam on an airplane to Malaysia, and the plane was shot down in Ukraine. One day, two hundred and ninety eight people perished. You didn't perish last year. You should look back and say Thank you Father, because I'm a potential victim in the hands of Satan, but because of the One that lives in me, I escaped everything.

Father, left to the devil I would not have escaped, but thank you for your mercy that allowed me to escape the entire year of 2014. I give glory to your name.

This year 2015 is the year God your father and my father has called our Year of Maximum. God doesn't do anything until He has said it. You many not hear it, you may not see it, you may not be able to discern it, but one way or the other He says it. He says it, sometimes to give people a chance to repent, and sometimes to allow somebody to stand in gap to avert the evil. The Bible says that said God would do nothing until he has told his servant, his prophets.

It is God's practice and principles, to say something before He does it. When He wanted to displace darkness, He said let there be light. He could have created light without speaking but because of His principles He had to say it.

What has God said concerning your 2015? He has called the year 2015, your Year of Maximum. He has said that you are leaving minimum, and going into your maximum. If I were you I would rejoice and praise Him.

Father, for what you have said, for what you have declared, for what you have proclaimed concerning my 2015, my Year of Maximum I am here to thank and exalt you. I am here to exalt you, for what you have said concerning my 2015.

Praise Him. If you understand the mystery of minimum you will know it's not good to have minimum. When you are living in "not enough" or "just enough", the prophecy of maximum can change your story; prophecy is a story changer.

Thank the Lord; because your story is changing in 2015, the story of your family and the story of His church is changing in 2015.

Using Matthew 4, I want to touch on a few things to help our understanding. When you get God's vision for your life of maximum, you will be eternally grateful. There is no way your story won't change by this prophecy. If you are at minimum, you eat from whatever falls off the master's table, you wait till others are full and eat from their left overs, but when you're at maximum, you take your portion.

I decree concerning your destiny, in the name of Yeshua the Son of God, the One who called the year 2015 your year of Maximum, you are going to the top in the name of Jesus Christ.

Jesus' life was tied to prophecy, everywhere He went, He was directed by prophesy. Matthew 4:12-16 gives us a great example, the scripture says,

When Jesus heard that John had been put in prison, he withdrew to Galilee. Leaving Nazareth, he went and lived in Capernaum, which was by the lake in the area of Zebulun and Naphtali— to fulfill what was said through the prophet Isaiah: "Land of Zebulun and land of Naphtali, the Way of the Sea, beyond the Jordan, Galilee of the Gentiles—the people living in darkness have seen a great light; on those living in the land of the shadow of death a light has dawned.

Prior to the prophecy being fulfilled, they were sitting in darkness and they were under the threat of death; but when the prophecy came to pass, their light came and their story changed.

Father, I thank you for the prophecy of 2015, my year of maximum; it is my game changer and my story changer.

Father, I thank you sincerely for the year 2015, my year of maximum. I thank you for the month January 2015, and for all the 31 days in the month.

Say, O January 2015, I thank God for you, because you will bring my way Maximum in every area of life.

Praise and thank Him, sow thanksgiving, so you can reap miracles this month.

May I say this to help you? Prayer is a seed. Why? Whatever you do today that can affect your tomorrow is a seed.

Baptize your January with thanksgiving, and let it be filled with thanks, so that all you will see this month are things that make you want to thank God.

You know, a companion you can't live without throughout your life is mercy of God. If mercy is not with you this year, you are in trouble, because nothing will fight for you but His mercy. That's why David the wise man prayed that goodness and mercy should follow him all the days of his life. The day mercy expires for you, that is the day you are leaving this earth because you have become exposed to everything. What defends a man in the land of the living is mercy. Once mercy is withdrawn you're done.

Father, in the year 2015 especially this month of January in this year of Maximum, beautify my life, beautify my family, beautify my destiny, beautify your church, beautify your people with

your mercy and your goodness in the name of Jesus.

The number 1, which January stands for is the number of new beginning. Ask the Lord, to give you a new story and a new beginning in January, let Him know you don't want to continue with the story of 2014.

Father, give me a new story, give me a new beginning, and give me a new start in the name of Jesus. Let it begin today. This month of January is the first month of this year; please change my beginning and my story in the name of Jesus Christ.

In Luke 5:1, we find the story of a man who was less than minimum, Jesus asked him to launch his nets into the deep for a drought. The man responded that he had toiled all night. Everyone who had a story of toiling in 2014, in the name of Yeshua the Son of God, you will have a new story in the name of Jesus Christ.

He was below capacity, he said we have toiled all night and caught nothing. See the conversation between Jesus and him, in verse 4-5 *now when he had left speaking, he said unto Simon, Launch out into the deep, and let down your nets for a draught. And Simon answering said unto him, Master, we have toiled all the night, and have taken nothing: nevertheless at thy word I will let down the net.*

How many nets did Jesus ask him to drop? He said "nets", but Peter determined his capacity. He was supposed to drop nets but he dropped a net. In the name of Jesus, may God give you divine expansion for capacity in the name of Jesus Christ.

Net instead of nets. They limited their capacity.

Father let fire destroy anything that will limit me in mentally and in my approach to life in the name of Jesus Christ.

Many of us are limited by the way we look at ourselves, may God tear by fire whatever wants to limit us internally.

Father whatever wants to limit me in my mental faculty, in my mind, in my heart, in my view, anything that Satan wants to use to limit me, tear it down by fire in the name of Jesus Christ. In my mindset, my heart-set, my view-set, in any area, in any way that Satan tells me oh no, someone like you cannot be there, O my Father, tear it by fire in Jesus mighty name we pray.

I want to help you to repeat that prayer. I said mindset, some things are friend-set, and some things are family-set. The brothers of David said he couldn't kill Goliath. David wanted to get to maximum his brothers said he could not. So family set, head-set, mind-set, friends-set, any set that wants to set me back from my maximum, Father roast it by fire.

Today is a major day in our lives and destinies, today we see God painting our lives with various results and outcomes that the world cannot deny.

All that concerns you is entering this dimension of blessing with you. This includes your destiny, family, home, marriage, career, business, and everything you represent in life. Everything that is linked to you is also entering this order with you.

Remember the story of Abraham, as reported by the book of Hebrews 11:9. It said, *While Abraham, Isaac and Jacob were in the same tent.* As Bible students, you know this never happened in the physical but everywhere Abraham was, his future was in him. Everywhere he was, everything he would ever become was also in him. Given this, as you stand, in the place of prayer this day, you are not the only one standing; destinies are in you, standing also with you. Lives are also standing with you. Businesses, careers, future promotions and mercy that are upon your generation are also standing with you.

I welcome you into your era of multiple portions. That is why the Bible uses the language "and the house of Jacob." Though it was Jacob who came, it was not just he alone standing there in God's presence. Everything that is in him was also standing there. Welcome into the place where all that is yours will be perfected in Jesus precious name. Being the first month of the year 2015, in our year of maximum, we are going to focus on the power of praise; the position praise takes not just to bring freedom, but also to bring a people into their era of maximum.

While many things are important, some are requirements. Something may be important without being a requirement. But if it is a requirement, it becomes very important. Praise is not just important it is a requirement to all living. I repeat Praise is a requirement for all living. The most important thing for every living being and the most required thing from every living being by God is their praise.

It is a requirement for all living beings to offer praise to the one that has preserved their soul Your praise is the most important thing that God requires from you and I. Isaiah 38:19 says, *the living, the living he shall praise thee, as I do this day.*

Praise is not what you do weekly, monthly or yearly, but something you do daily. If it must happen daily, it is a requirement. And for every day you live, you must remember what is required of you. You must know what God requires of you and if you meet God's requirements, the earth will have to make room for you.

When God said let there be light, there was light. The power of divine mandate required the appearance of light in the earth to take away darkness. In the same vein, the mandate on man to bring down praise on the earth is a requirement.

The same way that light showed up to take away darkness from the earth, is the same way praise should show up to take away demonic and darkness appearance on the earth. Your praise and my praise can take them away.

Psalm 67:5-6 says *let the people praise thee O God; let all the people praise thee. Then shall the earth yield her increase and God, even our own God, shall bless us.*

He said, *then shall the earth yield her increase.* The earth will make room for you when you make room for praise and as the living, you carry a mandate to make room for praise in your life, to make room for praise in your home, to make room for praise in the city of God and if we make room for praise, the earth must also make room for us. As you appear before your God, to make room for His praise today, may the earth make room for you in the name of Jesus Christ, Amen!

Understand this, when Lazarus died, according to John 11, there was no more room for him on the earth. Life does not make room for dead people. For this reason at the entrance to his tomb or his grave, there was a stone placed because his case was closed as long as the earth remained.

Jesus came to the grave of Lazarus, He asked them to take away the stone. They took the stone away, in order to make room for him on the earth so he can come out of the grave, and enjoy praise in the land of the living. What Jesus did was to make room for praise on behalf of Lazarus. As soon as Jesus lifted praise to heaven, on behalf of Lazarus, the earth had to make room for him. The door was shut against him because of death. Praise removed the door and the earth made room for him.

Life will make room for you if you make room for praise. Like we said before, praise is more than just singing. As you make room for praise, heaven and earth will make room for you.

Jesus said *Lazarus come forth!* The Bible said *he that was dead came forth,* and He said *loose him, and let him go* so he can take his place on the earth. Your praise is vital to where the earth places you. In this January may your place be secured because of your praise in the name of Jesus Christ, Amen!

I know this is the beginning of our journey in this year. You are protecting your future with your prayers. You are painting a color of how you want your year and future to appear.

The impact of your blessings (or praises) on the earth is tied to the intensity of your praise. When you take your praise to the maximum, the earth will be in awe of what God is doing with you to the maximum degree.

You cannot give him fearful praises and he won't give you fearful blessings. Then shall the earth yield her increase and God, even our God shall bless us. The earth will fear him. May your 2015 and your now be colored with fearful blessings in the name of Jesus Christ, Amen!

How do you enjoy that dimension of blessings? When you offer to him fearful praises. There is someone reading this book today whose story will make the world stand in awe of your God in the name of Jesus Christ. If you are the fellow, say a loud Amen!

In Psalm 67:4-5, the Bible says *O let the nations be glad ... for thou shall judge the people righteously, and govern the nations upon the earth. Let the people praise thee, O God; let all the people praise thee.* It is a requirement for the living. If you are one of His people you must understand this mandate and assignment you carry as a living being.

Let the people praise him. Let all the people, not some of the people, the maximum number of people that is available. All of them should praise Him. Then shall the earth yield her increase. And God, even our own God shall bless us.

In verse 7, the Bible says *God shall bless us; and all the ends of the earth shall fear him.* When you give Him fearful praise, He will give you fearful blessings. That is why Moses said in Exodus 15:11 *Who is like unto thee O Lord, among the gods? Who is like thee, glorious in holiness, fearful in praises, doing wonders?* His fearful praise released the "wonderbility" of God. When you offer Him a fearful praise, you release for yourself, for your destiny and future, a "wonderbility" of God.

May your life today, this week and the entire year be decorated with wonders in the name of Jesus Christ.

How do you enjoy such dimensions of wonders? By offering Him fearful praise. You provoke His ability of wonders, when you offer Him fearful praise. Fearful praises open the door of God's wonders to you.

You cannot offer Him fearful praise without Him giving you fearful blessings and wonders. Let's look at another scripture before we take time and give him to give Him fearful praise. In Exodus 15:6-11

Thy right hand, O LORD, is become glorious in power: thy right hand, O LORD, hath dashed in pieces the enemy. And in the greatness of thine excellency thou hast overthrown them that rose up against thee: thou sentest forth thy wrath, which consumed them as stubble. And with the blast of thy nostrils the waters were gathered together, the floods stood upright as an heap, and the depths were congealed in the heart of the sea. The enemy said, I will pursue, I will overtake, I will divide the spoil; my lust shall be satisfied upon them; I will draw my sword, my hand shall destroy them. Thou didst blow with thy wind, the sea covered them: they sank as lead in the mighty waters. Who is like unto thee, O LORD, among the gods? who is like thee, glorious in holiness, fearful in praises, doing wonders?

Every enemy pursuing you, the sea will cover them in the name of Jesus Christ. Amen!

Any one that said you will not enter your maximum and your freedom will sink like lead in the mighty name of Jesus.

You activate His wonder power by your glorious praise. You will lift up your voice and say to God:

Lord God Almighty, my Father and King. You preserved me, my household and your church throughout 2014 and to see January 2015. Father I am here to give you praise, to glorify you.

The mercies of God are new every morning. So far, you have enjoyed a dimension of His mercies totaling the number of days this year already through which you have not been consumed.

Father, for every daily mercy I, my family and your church and our land has enjoyed till this day, we are here to magnify you, to adore you, to lift you up. If not for your mercy, we should have been consumed. Therefore for the mercy we have enjoyed this year, we are here to say "Thank you".

His mercies are quantifiable. That is why the Bible says *they are new every morning.* Right now, you have seen several mornings this year already. His mercy showed up every morning. There was no morning God suspended his mercy for you, for me, your family and His church. Because mercy showed up, destruction moved back.

Father, for every destruction that you moved back for me, my family, your church and this

land, we are here to say, "Thank you". Visible and invisible destruction that you moved back, I am here to say thank you.

Romans 9:16 says So then *it is not of him that willeth, nor of him that runneth, but of God that sheweth mercy*. It means everything you have enjoyed this year came because of His mercy.

Father, for everything you gave me, my family and your church I say thank you. For everything you blessed me with, blessed my family with, and blessed your church with I say thank you.

Father, for every day I have enjoyed this year by your mercy I am here to say thank you.

His word says He has given us all things to enjoy. Everything you have enjoyed this year is because God gave them to you to enjoy.

In Hebrews 2:5, the Bible says *For unto the angels hath he not put in subjection the world to come, whereof we speak.*

He didn't hand over the power of the world to come to the angels but to man. We know this because in verse 6, it says *but one in a certain place testified, saying, what is man, that thou art mindful of him? or the son of man that thou visitest him?*

The world to come, the years to come He gave to man already, to us already. That is why men can say they are creating cars of 2015 in 2014 because the world to come is already in our hands. If you can create cars for 2015 in 2014, you can thank him for years and months in advance.

Father, for the entire year of 2015, my year of maximum especially the month of January, I thank you.

Father, today we say thank you, take all the praise, take all the honor. If we used the entire day to thank you, it will never be enough. Before we existed, men were praising you. While we are, they are still praising you, when we will not be any longer, the world and the earth will still be praising you but today as the living, we have come to thank you for preserving our souls.

We have escaped 2014. We have heard about what you want to do in 2015, our year of maximum, our ears have heard it, so our eyes will see it. Thank you for maximum. We're relocating from the bottom to the very top, from under to the top, from the tail to be the head; from down to the

top of the mountain, thank you for this divine relocation, we give you praise and thanks in the name of Jesus.

Today, as you open some truth to your people, on what will help them to know what to expect in 2015, Holy Father, open our eyes to understand scriptures in the name of Jesus Christ.

Holy Father, Holy Master, open our spirit man to understand prophesies in the name of Jesus Christ in Jesus mighty name we pray. Amen.

My ears have heard it, my eyes will see the maximum in this year 2015.

It is in God's practice, to let your eyes see what your ears have heard. 1 John 1:2-3. When you hear it, it's in His program for you to see it. I prophesy to you, everything your ears are hearing, your eyes will see in the name of Jesus Christ. Amen.

My Prayer for You This Month:

Our Father in heaven we thank you for preserving our souls, the souls of our family members and your church to see the first month of the year 2015, our year of maximum. We are here to offer you all our praises. You deserve them and we give them all to you in the name of Jesus Christ. Amen!

Lord as we go with this charge today, to give you thanks throughout today, to offer you praise while we work, move from one location to another, let our praises ascend up to heaven in the name of Jesus Christ.

As we offer to you fearful praise, may our lives experience wonders in the name of Jesus Christ. We dedicate both today and the entire year of 2015 especially January 2015 to you in the name of the Father, the Son, and the Holy Spirit. Thank you Almighty Father, glory be to your name in Jesus mighty name we pray. Amen!

Prayer Charge for January

One of my responsibilities today, on this opening day, is not just to bring you to prayers but to set expectations for you for 2015. Don't be confused about the reasons why we invest such time in prayer and fasting. Even the world has next year's miracles on the streets. The miracles of 2015 were already on the streets in 2014; 2015 car models were on the streets in 2014. This implies that those living in the world are living ahead of the church. The church does not understand that we are the ones who should be living such lives. Tasting the power of the Word to come.. When God explained that to me, He said the world is planning for the future more than the church. The church waits for it to come while the world goes to meet it.

By July of 2015, 2016 cars will be on the street. The engineering work is already on ground. I have a friend, who works for one of the auto companies. He shared with me that cars are made 5 years earlier; all they do is make minor changes to it, but the designs for those years are already completed. For some of us, we are still in our yesterday, talk less of tomorrow. But the world is ahead, no wonder scripture says in Luke 16:8 *the children of this world are in their generation wiser than the children of light.* But today we are reversing that story.

My assignment is to let you understand what to expect as your pastor, as your prophet, as your spiritual brother, as co-sons in this kingdom. You must understand what God wants to do with you, for you not to be stranded in life and to secure light for your journey. The virgins described in the Bible were virgins, but didn't get to the end of their journey, because they had no light to take them through the journey. The wise ones, had light. The use of oil is not to drink, it's to give light to your lantern. The foolish virgins asked the wise virgins to give them a little oil and they responded that they should go buy theirs, as it was not enough for all of them.

If you have light, you will have enough to go through life's journey, and the word of God is light to you. The Bible says in Psalm 119:105, *thy word is a lamp unto my feet. And a light unto my path.* Without light or His word, you will likely be stranded. That's why you need a word in your journey to enable you say to God, this is what I heard from you, you must sort me out. There is no one who has a word from Him, who can ever be stranded. The word, the light must bring you out. That's why I believe with the whole of my heart, in this 2015, you are relocating from the bottom, from the middle to the top in the name of Jesus Christ.

In Luke 24:44 *And he said unto them, These are the words which I spake unto you, while I was yet with you, that all things must be fulfilled, which were written in the law of Moses, and in the prophets, and in the psalms, concerning me.*

There are three books that contained prophecies about Jesus originally; the books of Moses, books of the prophets and the Psalms. All had to be fulfilled. Jesus didn't just live, prophecy helped him in life. If I must fulfill my assignment, prophecy spoken and written about me must be fulfilled. Every word of God concerning your maximum, as prophecy came to pass for Jesus; they will come to pass for you in the name of Jesus Christ.

Verse 45: *Then opened he their understanding, that they might understand the scriptures.*

There is a need for your understanding to be opened to understand prophecies, when you don't understand four things will likely happen to you, among which is you will underuse your opportunity. How many of us have some equipment at home that you don't understand how it works, you just use it for the common things: play, stop, pause, remind, and forward.

Lack of understanding makes you enjoy minimum benefits, when maximum benefits are available to you. Understanding is so crucial that the Bible counsels, with all thy getting, get understanding. Very important, without proper understanding, you will likely lose out from the major benefit that Heaven has ordained for you.

What does maximum mean? And I'll say the way it applies to you. Maximum can be defined as a state of greatness or the highest position allowable. Meaning if they allow human beings to get there, you can get there. In this 2015, if they allow people who are living to get there nothing is going to stop me and you. So, when you look at your career, look at what is allowable in your career. Look at your finances what maximum does your bank allow you to put in?

If they don't have a maximum, it means a lot of money must come into my account. Satan must not stop me because I must eat out of the riches of the glory of God by Christ Jesus.

Maximum also means to get to the very top in an organization. Have you heard the phrase "he has maxed out his credit card"? You know what it means. How many of us have heard that before? In 2015, I see you maxing up favor in the name of Jesus Christ. You will max out prosperity in the name of Jesus Christ. You will max out good health in the name of Jesus Christ, and you will max out promotion in the name of Jesus Christ.

It also means or denotes the highest point or amount attained.

If you don't know this higher level, you can't max out your life. You must know it to enjoy it. In fact there was a way God put it to me, He said "I don't determine their maximum, they determine their maximum. He said whatever they consider as their maximum, is what I will make their maximum. When the widow ran to Elisha in 2 Kings 4, he told her to go and borrow vessels, not a few. That was the instruction. He said when you come into the house fill the vessels with oil to the brim (maximum). Anyone that is full set it aside.

Let me ask you a question, who determined how much oil she had, God or her? When she said I have enough vessels, God said I have enough promotion for you. You are the one that will determine how far God takes you in 2015. You come with one vessel, heaven will fill one vessel, you come 1,000 vessels, and heaven will fill 1,000 vessels. Borrow vessels, not a few. And when they are full, set the full one aside. And the woman kept saying bring the vessels, the children said that's it, and the Bible said *and the oil stayed*. So, they determined how much they got.

Hear this, you cannot bankrupt God with your desire for maximum. No matter how much you are asking for, God won't run bankrupt. The Bible says of the fullness of his own grace; we are all eating from his "extra". We've not even touched the real thing. *He anointed my head, and my cup runneth over*. In this season of maximum, your cup will not just be full; your cup will overflow in the name of Jesus Christ.

Let me ask you a question, why would they fill a cup until it's running over? Because it's more than adequate from its source. If the source was inadequate, when you fill the cup up till the middle, you'll say it's enough, it's enough. If it's barely adequate, they will gauge it.

Pray and say: Father, I am leaving minimum and going to my maximum. Understand this is God's provision for you, the key word or scripture to hold onto is Joel 2:22, *Be not afraid, ye beasts of the field:*

for the pastures of the wilderness do spring, for the tree beareth her fruit, the fig tree and the vine do yield their strength.

It's tough to believe for you when you are below minimum and you are given a prophecy of maximum. You wonder how it will happen? This is what happened to the man called Zechariah in the Bible. This was someone who had not had a child for many years. The angel came and said you are going to have a son and of course the man was afraid. He was arguing even when the angel was talking and the angel had to make him dumb.

Sometimes some promises can be too much for you to handle. You have never had a child before, and following an ultrasound, the doctor tells you, "well I see triplets," you say, "It cannot be." One of my daughters, who recently had twins, said that during the ultrasound when the nurse told her it was twins, she just ignored it, and said to herself, how can it be twins. She said when she got home, and called the hospital, and said, "What did you tell me?" She could not believe she was having twins. There were no twins in her lineage. What is not in your lineage and family, may God bring it your way, in the name of Jesus Christ.

It's possible to be afraid when exposed to certain level of blessing. You've been living from paycheck to paycheck, but suddenly you become an employer of labor. You can be afraid. I prophesy to you, may my God give you fearful blessings in the name of Jesus Christ. He said, be not afraid, ye beast of the field, for the pasture of the wilderness to spring. If animals sleep in the wilderness, they should be afraid, because there are no pastures in the wilderness. But don't be afraid because in your wilderness your pasture will spring forth. Say, "in my wilderness my pasture will spring."

They are yielding to capacity, your strength is to capacity, and they're yielding to maximum.

You must go and find out what is allowable in your position. If that position is too small for you, say I think I need to change position.

For the fig and the vine, do yield their strength. You will not yield below your capacity in the name of Jesus Christ. Be not afraid, for the pastures of the wilderness do spring, the tree shall yield her fruit, the fig tree and the vine they will yield their strength.

Say to yourself, in this month of January 2015, and throughout the year 2015, I will yield my strength, I will yield my capacity. I will yield my maximum.

Chapter Two
February 2015

You are welcome again into the presence of God, the author and finisher of our faith. Nothing is made that was made without Him. Nothing can be made without God. If anything must be, it must be at the command of His word and approval. On all matters of life and issues of life he has the final say. Even Satan needs His approval to do anything.

We should feel privileged and opportune to have God as our Father. We must understand the size of our God to understand how privileged we are. Nothing was made that was made without Him. Everything that will happen occurs as approved by Him.

In the story of Job, Satan had attempted many times to touch Job but every time he found an edge around him that he couldn't penetrate. Satan has attempted to attack you several times but found the impenetrable edge of the Almighty around you. Every time he came to harm you, the edge of the Almighty was your protection. Without God's approval you will not be in the land of the living today. We would all have been forgotten. He has approved for us to be here and to be beneficiaries of His mercies and privileges in 2015, our year of Maximum.

Friends, you will never become what you have not confessed. The power to become is embedded in the power of confession. This is part of the ways of God. Moses knew His ways while the children of Israel knew His acts. When you know His ways you will create waves on the earth.

One of His ways you must know is that without confession you may never see what your heart desires. For the bible says, let the weak say I am strong - that is confession, you must say it. Without saying it, you cannot appropriate the blessing meant for your life.

Now confess – "2015, is My Year of Maximum".

You must confess it a lot so it resonates in your spirit and your spirit will be aligned with it.

May God cause this prophecy to enter your spirit man in the name of Jesus Christ.

First of all, thanksgiving is expected to be your first response to the word of God. When God wanted to give His best, He sent His word.

John 1:14 says *and the Word was made flesh, and dwelt among us, (and we beheld his glory, the glory as of the only begotten of the Father,) full of grace and truth.*

When God wants to bless His people, He sends His word to them. When the word is sent to you, your future is guaranteed. In the story of Joseph, he lived in chains until the word of God came. Every kind of struggle you are going through, may the word of God deliver you.

May His word bring about your breakthrough in Jesus Name.

Every promise from Him must raise praise from you. His promises must create praise out of your life.

It takes prayer to enforce God's will. The Bible instructs us to pray and say *thy kingdom come and thy will be done on earth as it is in heaven.* Without prayer, the will of God may be provided for you but be delayed getting to you.

May your prayer for 2015 remove delay from your life in the name of Jesus Christ. Daniel's continued prayer removed delay from his destiny.

May your prayer today cancel and eradicate every delay in the name of Jesus Christ.

Prayer is a seed. Whatever you do today that can affect your tomorrow is seed. This means, every prayer that has left your lips will have an effect on your life. Hannah prayed and the prayer left her mouth but on her return the following year, it was a different story. May every prayer you pray today beautify your 2015.

You must understand what God's plan is for your life. What is God's plan for your life? What work does He want to do?

What He wants to do is to make sure that your life enters into its dimension of divine maximum. The Lord said in Isaiah 45:11, *concerning the work of my hand, command ye me.* This means there is something God wants to do in your life.

God wants to do a surgery of maximum in your life. You have to understand what He wants to do; He wants to work on your destiny. He wants to take you from minimum to maximum, from the bottom to the top. May God take you from where you are to your maximum dimension in the name of Jesus Christ.

Jabez was at his minimum in his family. From the beginning of his life all he knew was minimum but prayer changed his story. By your prayers this month and this year, may God relocate you from your minimum point to your maximum in Jesus Name.

Today becomes the day of change for you in the name of Jesus Christ, Amen.

How long it has been does not matter, what matters is to understand what God wants to do.

In John 5, Jesus asked the man if he would be made whole. He began to tell stories. Rather than stories, simply indicate whether you want to relocate from minimum to maximum. God needs your consent to bless you.

Where you have been does not matter, what matters to God is what He wants to do with you.

Lift up your voice and thank Him for what He wants to do in your life.

Father, I am here to thank you because I'm part of your plan for 2015, especially the month of February.

The thoughts I think towards you are thoughts of good and not evil to give you an expected end (Jeremiah 29:11).

What are His thoughts towards you in 2015? To make everything that concerns you good in 2015.

Father, for your thoughts for me, your plans for my life, my family and your church to bring me to maximum in 2015, I am here to say thank you in the mighty name of Jesus.

Father, thank you for bringing everything that concerns me in 2015 into maximum in the name of Jesus.

Every time His word comes to a people, they are no longer whom they were. For Joseph when his word came, he was transformed from a servant to a Lord. There is a Lord, a greatness in you that the word of God will bring out in you in the year of maximum.

Father, for what the word will bring out, what I will become in the year of maximum, I am here to say thank you in the mighty name of Jesus.

A new you is emerging in 2015. Whatever God has ordained to be in your life that is yet to be manifested, is coming out in year 2015.

The Bible says, *Touch not mine anointed, and do my prophets no harm. Moreover he called for a famine upon the land: he brake the whole staff of bread. He sent a man before them, even Joseph, who was sold for a servant:*
Until the time that his word came: the word of the Lord tried him. The king sent and loosed him; even the ruler of the people, and let him go free. He made him lord of his house, and ruler of all his substance: (Psalm 105:15-17,19-21).

Confess: My word has come to me, that the year 2015 is my year of maximum.

The word changes who you are not just your situation.

Father, for the new me that will emerge, for my new family, new career, new destiny, new church that will emerge in 2015 I am here to say thank you.

In this year 2015, all these prophecies will come to past, we have been given permission to call the things that be not as though they were.

In Psalm 115:12, David mentioned something that I want you to consider, and that is also your story. *The LORD hath been mindful of us: he will bless us; he will bless the house of Israel; he will bless the house of Aaron.* Meaning we are in His heart, we are in His agenda, that is why the Bible says "the Lord has been mindful of us. He will bless us."

Father, I thank you because you are mindful of me, you are mindful of my family, you are mindful of my destiny and you are mindful of your church. Who am I, what am I, that you are mindful of me and my family, we thank you oh my

father. Blessed be your name, glory be to your name, in Jesus mighty name we pray.

You can never win the race of life without mercy. Life will punish you without mercy. Life was hard and tough on blind Bartimeus until mercy came. When Jesus came, mercy located him.

Father, in February 2015 and throughout 2015, baptize me oh Lord with your mercy in the mighty name of Jesus.

Life's journey is sweet when mercy is on your side. Jacob said if not because of the mercy of God, the tender mercy of God with me, I crossed here with a stick. That's minimum. He had nothing, just a stick. He was so broke, he was broken. Some of you travel, and have excess luggage, he didn't have luggage, only one stick, but when he was returning, because mercy followed him on the journey, he had excess.

You want to pray to God, in this year of Maximum, especially February, let mercy follow me, let it follow me in this journey, don't let mercy leave me alone.

Father in the year 2015 especially in the month of February, O mercy of God, follow me, everywhere I go, follow me. Follow me,

everywhere I go, in the air, in the sea, the word of God says goodness and mercy shall follow me, Mercy follow me all thorough this year 2015, especially in the month of February. Blessed be your name, in Jesus mighty name we pray.

One other thing you want mercy to do for you is to defend you. When the enemy comes against you, even when you are at fault, mercy must rise for you.

Father, throughout 2015 especially in February let mercy defend me, let mercy fight for me, in the name of Jesus. O my father, I need your mercy, let it defend me, let it fight for me, let it not fight against me, but fight for me, fight for my family, fight for my household, fight for your people O Lord, let mercy fight for us, let mercy defend us, in the name of Jesus.

Everywhere we go, everywhere we turn let mercy defend us. Blessed be your name oh Lord, thank you Father, in Jesus precious name we pray. Amen.

The number two is the number of fruitfulness. The power of fruitfulness is embedded in the number 2. *And He blessed them, and said be fruitful.*

You are going to cry to February and say, February you are number two, you are my month to be fruitful, all through February I shall be fruitful, I will multiply I will expand.

Father, I decree concerning February, O February of 2015, bring me fruitfulness, multiply me, increase me, enlarge my coast in the name of Jesus. O February hear the word of the Lord, you are my month to bring me fruitfulness, I will be fruitful, I will enlarge, I will increase in the name of Jesus. Blessed be your name O Lord, in Jesus mighty name we pray.

Father, in the name of Jesus, I prophesy concerning February, Oh February, 2nd month of the year, bring me fruitfulness, bring me increase, and bring me enlargement, in the name of Jesus. Blessed be your name, thank you Father, in Jesus mighty name we pray.

The month of February is a month of "2", it must operate in the dimension of number 2. Scripture says that one will chase a thousand but two will put ten thousand to flight. Your month of February must produce better and greater results than January.

Father, my February will be better than my January from the first day to the last day in the mighty name of Jesus.

The number two is the number of assistance. You will not lose whatever assistance you need to get to your maximum.

Two are better than one; because they have a good reward for their labour (Ecclesiastes 4:9).

Father, all through the month of February 2015 and the entire year of 2015, every assistance and help I need to enter into my maximum, Lord send them my way in the name of Jesus.

In 2 Chronicles 26:15, the Bible said Uzziah was marvelously helped till he reached his maximum

Father, throughout the month of February 2015 and the entire year of 2015, send men to help me marvelously until I get to my maximum in Jesus mighty Name.

The Bible says the evil of a day is sufficient for it thereof. Every day has the potential for evil.

O February 2015 and throughout the year 2015, whatever evil you carry must not come near me, my family, my career, your church in the name of Jesus.

Pray in the Holy Ghost for a minute.

My Prayer For You This Month:

Father we thank you so much for the privilege to see the second month in the year 2015. We honor you; we glorify you.

The art of preservation is your doing and yours only. You don't have a co-worker. You are the only one that can preserve. For preserving us, we honor you. For all you have planned for us in 2015 especially in the month of February, take all the glory in the mighty name of Jesus. May your mercy that advances life's journey be adequate maximally for us in the mighty name of Jesus.

King of Glory, we want maximum mercy in the year 2015 especially February 2015. Release it to us in the name of Jesus Christ, Amen.

As your people have prayed, let every prayer receive immediate attention in the mighty name of

Jesus Christ. Father, exempt us from whatever evil is in February 2015, in the name of Jesus Christ.

We vow all the glory and praise to you, thank you Holy Father. Again we dedicate the month of February 2015 to you in the name of the Father, the son and the Holy Spirit. In Jesus mighty name we pray. Amen!

Prayer Charge for February

Anytime you shout Hallelujah, it's a threat to your enemies. Your enemies must be afraid of you in 2015. You use your shouting to terrorize them. The Bible says when Israel shouted; the philistines said woe unto us, for the God of the Hebrews has appeared for them. In this 2015, may your enemies curse themselves in the name of Jesus Christ. Shout a loud Hallelujah.

Praise is one of your secrets to enjoy maximum. Why? John 12:32 says, *And I, if I be lifted up from the earth, I will draw all men unto me.*

If I offer him maximum praise, I am sure he will give me maximum lifting. One area, to upgrade in your life in 2015 is your praise life. You must sing more, you must praise more, you must dance more, you must worship more, you must celebrate more, because the more you lift him up, the more He will lift you also. A man cannot be deeper than how much he has lifted God; your depth in life is determined by how much you have lifted Him. *And I, if I be lifted up from the earth, I will then draw all men unto me* (John 12:32). Determine to max out praise, so that God can max out miracles for you.

We prayed a prayer earlier in this chapter that when the word of Joseph came, the word didn't just change his circumstances, it also changed his personality. Before his word, he was a servant and when his word came, he became a ruler. You want to thank God for what you are going to become in 2015. There is something you're going to become that will surprise you. You will say, is this me? You will not only surprise yourself; you will surprise your neighbors also.

Let me show you a secret that your day can be addressed with. When God made all the days, the Bible says He said they were good. And on the seventh day, the Bible said, and concerning the seventh day, God blessed it, meaning you can bless your day. And if you can bless your day, then you can bless your week, your month and your year. You are going to decree concerning February one more time, and say O February you will make me fruitful, you will bring me to prosperity, and you will bring me to my maximum.

Let me show you another scripture. In Job 3:1-2, see what Job said concerning his own day.

After this opened Job his mouth, and cursed his day. And Job spake, and said, Let the day perish wherein I was born, and the night in which it was said, there is a man-child conceived.

If Job cursed his day, what should you do to your day. You can address your day, that's what I'm telling you. Just as he opened his mouth, you're going to open your mouth and bless all the days of the month of February all 28 days. Job cursed his birthday and until he changed his word, his world was very, very bad. But he began to change his word in chapter 41 of Job and by chapter 42 his story changed, because your word determines your world. As long as he kept cursing his world, his life was going down, but in chapter 41 he changed his word, his story changed in chapter 42, and his latter days were better than his beginning thereof.

You're going to call on every day of the month February, and say O February, hear ye the word of the Lord, this is the word of God you are blessed.

Father, I prophesy, as I open my mouth regarding February 2015, and the entire year I am blessed, I am promoted, I am lifted, I am enlarged, go ahead and prophesy to yourself. O February you carry 28 days, I am addressing every day of

February as I open my mouth, I am blessed, I will prosper, I will be rich, I will be wealthy, I will increase, I will be enlarged, I will be promoted, I will be lifted, I will be favored, I will be assisted, until I become very strong. My family shall also benefit, they will increase in the name of Jesus, every member of my household shall reach the top, they shall enjoy maximum, they shall reach their goal, they shall reach their top, in the name of Jesus, all of our days of February and throughout the year, in the name of Jesus. Blessed be your name oh Lord, Alleluia to you, in Jesus precious name we pray.

We said earlier that God had explained to you, what He wants to do with you in 2015, just as a surgeon explains to you the sort of procedure they want to have on you. God's procedure on you is procedure of maximum. He wants to do surgery, to put in you what will make you go to maximum. This Surgeon General, Jesus, wants to work on your destiny. You're going to tell God, I give my destiny to you, take me to my maximum, work on my destiny. Until he worked on Adam, he didn't produce Eve. You are going to tell God, work on my destiny.

Father, you are the Surgeon General of Heaven look down from heaven work on my

destiny, work on my life, work on my family, work on your church, and take us to maximum. Tell God to work on you. Have your way O Lord, work on me. My destiny must not remain this way, work on me, work on my home, and work on my marriage. Blessed be your name O Lord, thank you Father in Jesus mighty name we pray.

Scripture said by a prophet, Israel came out of Egypt, which was their lowest point and by a prophet, they were preserved; preserved to their highest point, which is Canaan. I therefore decree, wherever you are that will not allow you to enter maximum in life, I remove you from there in the name of Jesus Christ.

Wherever life has put in you that will not ensure that your life enjoys maximum, I bring you out in the name of Jesus Christ. I say, come out in the name of Jesus Christ. Not tomorrow, but today, walk out in the name of Jesus Christ, I place your feet prophetically upon the ladder of heaven that ensures your smooth ride to your maximum, therefore in the name of Jesus of Nazareth, keep moving higher in the name of Jesus.

Move higher, in the name of Jesus Christ, I say move higher in the name of Jesus Christ, whatever evil has partnered with 2015, whatever evil has promised 2015, I decree that those evil they will not come near your dwelling in the name of Jesus Christ.

You will not know them in the name of Jesus Christ, you will not see them in the name of Jesus Christ, and they will not come near you in the name of Jesus Christ. 2015 is evil-free for you in the name of Jesus Christ. Your joy shall be full. It shall be well with you. Amen!!

Chapter Three
March 2015

We welcome everyone into the presence of God, where we come to secure a future for ourselves based on the platform of His word, purpose, plan and prophecy.

Everyone who needed a change of tomorrow, who needed a different outcome, and who didn't like the way his or her life was going and wanted a new tomorrow changed it using the instrument of prayer. This means prayer is a forum for change, which means every time one comes to pray, one has come to the place of change.

Job 14:14b *all the days of my appointed time will I wait, till my change comes*. It takes prayer to wait on Him, and as you wait know that a change will come.

I prophesy to someone today, regarding your 2015, every change 2014 did not bring your way, 2015 will secure it for you in the name of Jesus Christ.

Prayer is an avenue for change, there is nothing you need changed in your current situation that prayer couldn't ensure to give you a better tomorrow. The man, Blind Bartimaeus was described by his condition; whatever condition is being used to describe you today, your prayer for 2015 will secure the change you need, in the Name of Jesus Christ.

Hannah, wanted a change, she was fed up of her current condition. There appeared no apparent change ahead of her. Instead of just crying and complaining she went and prayed. *And she was in bitterness of soul, and prayed unto the LORD, and wept sore* (1 Samuel 1:8-10). Whatever you desire for yourself, your family and the church of God, your quickest guarantee to receive it is by your prayer.

Jesus said in Matthew 11:24, *Therefore I say unto you, what things soever ye desire, when ye pray, believe that ye receive them, and ye shall have them.* This means my future is expressed in my prayer.

Jesus said in order for your joy to be full, you will need to ask. The scripture says *in everything by prayer and supplication and thanksgiving* (Philippians 4:6).

Every area of my life can have a secured future if I put it in prayer. James 4:2 *says yet ye have not, because ye ask not.*

The place of prayer is the place of birth. You come to birth your destiny. Jabez started as a minimum but his story had a better end. He secured himself a future through prayers

Let your faith regarding your tomorrow rise up, knowing that your effort over your life, and your 2015 is not a wasted effort. If you ask for it, God is too faithful to ignore the prayers of His children, Isaiah 49:15 *Can a woman forget her sucking child, that she should not have compassion on the son of her womb? yea, they may forget, yet will I not forget thee.* It means if He will not forget you, then your future is secured. It is a future that you have not prayed about, that you will not realize. Issues that were once a prayer point will become a praise report. John was once a prayer point in the life of Zechariah and Elizabeth and became a praise report.

God's prophecy is His word and His word is His will. *We have also a more sure word of prophecy; whereunto ye do well that ye take heed* (2 Peter 1:19). Prophecy is the will of God, the plan, agenda of God. And if it is His will, there is a guarantee that God will enforce His will.

And this is the confidence that we have in him, that, if we ask any thing according to his will, he heareth us: And if we know that he hear us, whatsoever we ask, we know that we have the petitions that we desired of him (1 John 5:14-15).

Knowing you are in the will of God stretches your confidence. Every request is answerable if it is under His will. His word is His will, and the prophecy spoken by Him is His will. It's a win-win situation for you, but you may never see it if you don't ask. You must ask and until you ask it will not become a possession for you.

In Luke 2, we see story of Simeon, God foretold about Jesus through many prophets but Simeon kept praying to enjoy this. Everything God has promised you, you will see in this land of the living in the name of Jesus Christ.

2015 is your year of maximum. Whatever is in your life and does not reflect maximum must obey the word of God in the name of Jesus Christ. May God ensure whatever change you need for your future in the name of Jesus Christ.

Unto him that is able to do exceedingly abundantly above all. It is unto Him that we pray.

Lift your voice and bless God

Thank Him for His plans for your future, Jeremiah 29:11 says *For I know the thoughts that I think toward you, saith the LORD, thoughts of peace, and not of evil, to give you an expected end.*

Father, I thank you for the future you have for me, my family, my loved ones and your church in the year 2015 especially in the month of March.

Father, for all I know, for the things I know that you have done already concerning my 2015, I am here to say thank you.

Thank you for everything you have done concerning my 2015, what you have set up concerning my January, February and March. For all you have done, I thank you. Thank you for lifting me up, for giving me maximum. The year 2015 is my year of maximum. I know eyes have not seen it, but I know you have done it. Blessed be your name O Lord, to you be all the praise O Lord, in Jesus mighty name we pray.

The month of March has 31 days. Psalm 68:19 says *Blessed be the Lord, who daily loadeth us with benefits, even the God of our salvation.* This means, every one of the 31 days is carrying benefits for you. *1 Corinthians 2:9 But as it is written, Eye hath not seen, nor ear heard, neither have entered into the heart of man, the things which God hath prepared for them that love him.* God has prepared something for this year for you and I, He has prepared something that eyes have not seen, nor ears heard.

Father, for what you have prepared for my 2015, especially the month of March, for what you have prepared for my family, my loved ones and

your church, I am here to thank you, in the name Jesus Christ.

One thing is very important to every living thing, and can't be over emphasized. This is the blessing of Mercy. If you have it, your life is secured. David understood this in Psalm 23:6 *that goodness and mercy shall follow me all the days of my life.* Without mercy, you are a potential victim in the hands of the devil. Mercy shields you, lifts you up, and fights your battles. This is why the blind man only asked for mercy when he realized Jesus was passing through.

Father, in this year 2015 release mercy upon me, my family, my loved ones and your church in the name of Jesus Christ.

May the God of all mercy have mercy on you in the name of Jesus Christ, Amen!

You want to cover your entire 2015 in the blood of Jesus. Revelations 12:11 says *And they overcame him by the blood of the Lamb.* Many of you will travel by the air, road, and sea. Not all journeys are favorable but when the blood of Jesus is covering you, it becomes favorable because the blood of Jesus speaks better things than the blood of Abel.

O March 2015, and the entire year of 2015 I cover you in the blood of Jesus.

The number 3 is the third month, which is the number of divine agreement. *For there are three that bear record in heaven, the Father, the Word and the Holy Ghost: and these three are one* (1 John 5:7). Ask Heaven to be in agreement with your Maximum. If Heaven is in agreement, the earth must cooperate, your career must cooperate, all must agree.

Father, may Heaven and Earth agree for my maximum, my family and loved ones' maximum in the name of Jesus Christ.

Then shalt thou go on forward from thence, and thou shalt come to the plain of Tabor, and there shall meet thee three men going up to God to Bethel, one carrying three kids, and another carrying three loaves of bread, and another carrying a bottle of wine:

And they will salute thee, and give thee two loaves of bread; which thou shalt receive of their hands (1 Samuel 10:3-4).

The number 3 is the number of what we call "unusual favor". May God give you unusual favor in the name of Jesus Christ, Amen. May the year 2015 cause your life and destiny to go forward in the name of Jesus Christ.

As we see above, the three people going to Bethel were meant to share three loaves of bread, but they came to an agreement to give Saul two loaves. That is unusual favor.

In the year 2015, especially in the month of March, let me, my family, loved ones and your church enjoy unusual favor. Let my career, business, ministry and all that concerns me enjoy unusual favor in the name of Jesus Christ.

And the LORD appeared unto him in the plains of Mamre: and he sat in the tent door in the heat of the day; And he lift up his eyes and looked, and, lo, three men stood by him (Genesis 18:1-2)

The scripture shows that the number 3 represents "divine visitation." This visitation took Sarah from barrenness to motherhood. Three men visited Sarah from God.

Father, in this month of March 2015, and the entire year of 2015, I will enjoy divine visitation that will change my story in the name of Jesus Christ.

Father, by divine visitation, change my story in 2015 especially in the month of March. O let my story change, in this 2015. By this visitation, change my story, you're the story-changer, visit me O Lord. Blessed be your name O Lord, thank you father, in Jesus mighty name we pray.

My Prayer for You This Month:

Our Father in heaven, we bless your name again for the privilege to be alive and to see the month of March 2015. For these and many more things you will do for us, accept our thanks in the name of Jesus.

For your thoughts to us in 2015, the year of maximum accept our thanks in the name of Jesus Christ. Your people have requested for mercy. Have mercy upon us in the name of Jesus Christ.

Make every prayer point, become a praise report in the name of Jesus Christ. Before today is over, let someone have an amazing testimony in the name of Jesus.

We vow all the glory and praise to you in Jesus name. We therefore dedicate the entire month of March 2015 to you in the name of the Father, the Son and the Holy Spirit. Thank you father, in Jesus Precious name we pray, Amen!!

Prayer Charge for March

We must understand the mindset of Abraham. While he had not seen Isaac, he did not consider his body that was now dead. The body was dead but he didn't see that. He was giving glory to God, though he had not seen it.

Don't wait till you see it before you believe it. Blessed is he who has not seen, but yet believe. Neighbor, I don't know about you, my case in March and the rest of 2015 is settled already. *He considered not his body now dead ... neither yet the deadness of Sara's womb... but was strong in faith, giving glory to God* (Romans 4:19-20).

He was strong, and he was already giving glory to God. It is important for you to know that He has already done it, so you will have the motivation to praise Him. Just so you know, what will happen this month will baffle your destiny.

Don't just live in 2015, see yourself operating in the level of the word of God, the word Maximum. You have to understand scriptures, while we look not at things which are seen, for the things which are seen are temporal, the things which cannot be seen are eternal, another translation says they are more real. Don't forget what we see today, was made by a God who was not seen. The invisible made the visible. The visible will appear from the invisible.

Moses was standing on a ground and God said in Exodus 3:5, *put off thy shoes from off thy feet, for the place whereon thou standest is holy ground.* If Moses didn't remove his shoe, it would have meant he didn't believe God. He removed his shoes, because it was not the normal place he was before, things had changed. There is a way you act when things have changed, Moses did not ask God when it changed to holy ground. He immediately removed his shoes, because where he was standing was now Holy Ground.

Father, I'm excited, thankful, and grateful for March 2015, for all you have done from the 1st day to the 31st day. Go ahead and praise the Lord. Give him thanks, for each day, the 1st day to the 31st day.

Earlier, we showed that in Genesis 18:2, the number 3 is the number of divine visitation, when three appeared to the man Abram. From that day Abram, became Abraham.

Three is a number of change. Whatever you expect to change, by this visitation, God will change for you in the name of Jesus Christ. When they met his wife Sarai, she became Sarah. Listen to me, once your name changes it means your identity has changed, whatever needs to be changed for you, may this year 2015 usher in your change in the name of Jesus Christ.

I declare under the order of the number 3, your own visitor that will change your story will visit you this month in the name of Jesus Christ. Some visitors come to add problems to your life, but I decree the visitors that will improve you, that will increase you, and enlarge you will visit you in the name of Jesus Christ.

And Elimelech Naomi's husband died; and she was left, and her two sons. And they took them wives of the women of Moab; the name of the one was Orpah, and the name of the other Ruth: and they dwelled there about ten years. And Mahlon and Chilion died also both of them; and the woman was left of her two sons and her husband. Then she arose with her daughters in law that she might return from the country of Moab: for she had heard in the country of Moab how that the LORD had visited his people in giving them bread. Wherefore she went forth out of the place where she was, and her two daughters in law with her; and they went on the way to return unto the land of Judah (Ruth 1:3-7)

God had not visited the land of Moab in ten years, but a particular year, their story changed. For ten years, their story was a sad one; it was a story of death. However, one day their story took a new turn. In the name of Yeshua the Son of God, 2015 will record for you a new story for every story that has remained the same for you in the past years, in the name of Jesus Christ.

Naomi heard that God was visiting somewhere. The world will hear that God is visiting you and your family in the name of Jesus Christ. For God had visited His people in giving them bread. Bread is not just what you eat, bread stands for what meets your needs. That is why He says *when ye pray, say give us this day, our daily bread*. Whatever you will need in 2015, when you receive your visitation, bread must come with it.

When Abraham and Sarah were visited, what they needed came with the visitation. What they needed was Isaac. You know Isaac was not just a child, Isaac was a promise and a covenant, so don't look at Isaac like a boy. He was a boy in the flesh, in the spirit he was a covenant. Out of him, the first twins that was ever to be born was coming out, and they were not just children, they were nations. God said *two nations are in your womb*.

So when you are looking at the story of Abraham and you say, Isaac, we are not talking about a person, we are talking about a destiny, because some of you will say, I don't want children, we're not talking about children now. You have to understand spiritual things. When God visited them, He visited them with their promise.

Whatever promise you are waiting for, 2015 will bring it to you in the name of Jesus Christ.

Some of you, have been hearing God say you will become millionaires, some of you have been seeing money in your dreams, and you wake up there is no money. I told you one day, I was spending in the dream, I woke up and said I want to go back to sleep but it was Sunday morning. I'm still waiting for the money, but I have seen it. We have seen ourselves in the glory days. This is not what we looked like in the revelation we saw, we were brighter, more beautiful, more glorious, wealthier that what we are seeing right now.

Abraham could not continue in covenant until his promise came. If Isaac did not come, there will be a discontinuity of promise in his life, that is why he was worried and he asked God in Genesis 15 whether his servant Eliezer would take all he had, because there had to be a continuity of covenant.

May God visit you and cause your promise to come to pass in the name of Jesus Christ.

Father, in this 2015, especially the month of March visit me with the promise. Lift your voice and pray that prayer.

Another thing the number 3 stands for is the power not to be held back. That is why the grave could not hold Jesus. On the 3rd, day He rose from the dead. Whatever has held you back before, as you appear in this month of March, they are losing the battle in the name of Jesus Christ.

Listen, the grave lost battle over the life of Jesus, over His destiny. Whatever has been oppressing you before, whatever has kept you under before has lost its battle in Jesus name.

When Jesus left the grave, He went to the maximum height. The Bible says for this purpose, God has highly exalted Him and given Him a name, which is above every other name. The number 3 ushered Him into that dimension. May this month of March, usher you to the highest level you can ever dream about in the name of Jesus Christ.

Father, in the year 2015 especially in the month of March, whatever has held me back, in the name of Jesus lose your grip, lose your hold, lose your power over my destiny, in the name of Jesus.

The Bible said for they heard that God has visited His people in giving them bread.

Father, in this year 2015, especially in the month of March, give me a visitation that the

world will hear about. Blessed be your name O Lord, thank you Father, in Jesus mighty name.

The number 3 is the number of the Holy Ghost; who is leader of the 3rd dispensation. In 2015, you must ask God to pour His Spirit upon you like never before.

Nobody carries the Spirit of God and lose battles. Impossible. Even when Samson, was in sin, as long as the Spirit of God was upon him, he was winning battles. His problem began, when the Holy Spirit walked out. He won't walk out of you in Jesus name.

You will not tamper with whatever will cause the Holy Spirit to leave you, in the name of Jesus Christ.

When Samson was coming out of the house of a harlot, they said to him, Samson, your enemies are upon you and locked up the gate. You know what he did? He carried the gate. Can you imagine? He wanted to teach them a lesson, he took the gate and said follow me. If somebody carried the gate, will you fight them? Somebody wants to beat you up, but before he beats you he starts by carrying your car, what would you do? I would not bother calling 911 because he might beat all the police officers. That was what Samson did. He could do that because the Spirit of God was in him, but when the Spirit of God walked out, even chickens made him afraid. The

Philistines removed his eyes, and they said Samson you need to dance, we have special number for you. He became a ridicule, to the extent that he died with his enemies on the same day, because the Spirit of God had left him.

Father, whatever I will do that will make your Holy Spirit leave me, O my Lord, have mercy on me, and may I never do it. Whatever that will make me sin against the Spirit, may I never do it in Jesus mighty name.

In this year 2015, Father, fill me with your Spirit to maximum, to overflow. I need a fresh power of your Holy Spirit.

Father, baptize me with fresh fire of the Holy Ghost in the year 2015, especially in the month of March. I need fresh fire, of the Holy Ghost, where the devil cannot stand in Jesus mighty name.

On the second day He will revive us, on the third day He will raise us up. All these destinies, on this third day, raise them up in the name of Jesus Christ.

Sometimes economic status gives you maximum, sometimes marriage status gives you maximum. Maximum that the world can't contain, that the world can't put limit on, grant to all these ones in the name of Jesus Christ. Let all the things they have read, let it become their experience in the name of Jesus Christ.

We dedicate March unto you, in the name of the Father, in the name of the Son, and the Holy Spirit. Thank you for settling March in Jesus name we pray.

Chapter Four
April 2015

I welcome everyone again into the presence of the One who fights the battle for our future.

A man cannot have a glorious future without a need to fight over his future. Every future, depending on the type of glory or star tied to the future, will have to battle through the kingdom of darkness.

The good news is that the One who created the future is more than enough to fight for His people. Every glorious and colorful future will go through one warfare or another.

The scripture says in 2 Chronicles 20:15 *the battle is not yours but God's.*

Even in the natural, airplanes that fly in the air at maximum and cars that drive on the ground at maximum do not experience the same turbulence. If you are a high flier in destiny you will experience more turbulence than the person whose destiny is on the ground.

One thing is secure; people who have their destiny in Him do not lose any battle. 1 John 5:4 says *for whatsoever is born of God overcometh the world; and this is the victory that overcometh the world, even our faith.* No matter how fierce the battle is, before it starts, you have been declared a winner.

You have come to His presence to fortify your destiny, so that your destiny will keep rising and Satan will not be able to do anything about it.

When they left Egypt, the Israelites went through different battles for over 400 years (generations average about thirty years in-between) but when God appeared for them, Egypt could not hold them anymore. In 2015, the God of the Hebrews is appearing for you in the name of Jesus Christ, Amen!

The number four (April, being the fourth month is represented by the number 4) is the number of Divine intervention in warfare.

When Nebuchadnezzar put the boys in the fiery furnace it was warfare against their God, against their destiny.

I declare that every fire against you will not harm you in Jesus name. If they have hurt you in the past, they will cease today in the name of Jesus Christ.

Then Nebuchadnezzar the king was astonished ... Did we not cast three men bound in into the midst of fire? ... I see four men loose ... and the form of the fourth is like the Son of God (Daniel 3:24-25).

The ***fourth man*** appeared for them. May the fourth man, the Man of War, appear to deliver you today in Jesus name. In every attempt of Satan to prevent you from shinning, he will lose that battle in Jesus name.

For 400 years, Egypt kept them down but when the God of the Hebrews was tired, He came down for them.

I prophesy: God is tired of seeing the way your life is going, He is coming down to rescue you today in the name of Jesus Christ.

One of the challenges in warfare over destiny is that it makes you question the promises of God. Even when Moses was taking the people out of Egypt they questioned where God was. He even had to ask God "What will I tell these people?" Every Egypt that has swallowed your faith will vomit it again in the name of Jesus Christ.

When you don't believe you don't get anything. *And blessed is she that believed: for there shall be a performance of those things, which were told her from the Lord* (Luke 1:45).

And Moses said unto the people, Fear ye not, stand still, and see the salvation of the LORD, which he will shew to you today: for the Egyptians whom ye have seen today, ye shall see them again no more forever. The LORD shall fight for you, and ye shall hold your peace (Exodus 14:13-14). This occurred when they started doubting the God of Covenants.

Moses knew the hold that Egypt had upon the lives of the Israelites was strong, and they struggled with believing him. May God punish whatever has affected your belief in the name of Jesus Christ.

The greatest thing a thief can steal is your faith. Once your faith is stolen, all your blessings are stolen with it. *For let not that man think that he shall receive any thing of the Lord* (James 1:7).

God told Moses when they ask who has sent you say the God of their fathers: Abraham, Isaac and Jacob has sent you.

May God do whatever your faith needs, so it can believe in the name of Jesus Christ.

I decree concerning you: In this land of the living you will see all that God has promised you in the name of Jesus Christ.

Out of all the sons of Jacob, Joseph was the most important; he was the last birth that his mother saw. After his birth, with the next birth, she died. He was the last joy his mother celebrated. An unusual favor of his Father that could not be explained was upon him.

I decree concerning you: In this 2015, especially this month of April, men will favor you in a way you cannot explain in Jesus name.

Your destiny determines the type of favor you attract. Satan is more interested in your destiny because you have a colorful destiny.

You are winning every fight over your destiny hands down today in the name of Jesus.

Because of the unusual favor there was warfare in his (Joseph) own household; none of the plots against him succeeded. Even the ones that seemed to succeed, God turned for his good.

Every plot against your destiny planned for evil, will work for your good in the name of Jesus Christ. Even the ones that seem to have succeeded will work for your good in the name of Jesus Christ. *And we know that all things work together for good to them that love God, to them who are the called according to his purpose* (Romans 8:28).

Who could have seen Joseph in his elevated position of maximum and say he had suffered?

Your enemy will be disappointed in the name of Jesus Christ. Let me announce to you: It is dangerous for anyone to set themselves as your enemy moving forward. God who sent me to you will rise against them in the name of Jesus.

Your destiny will determine your warfare. *There hath no temptation taken you but such as is common to man: but God is faithful, who will not suffer you to be tempted above that ye are able; but will with the temptation also make a way to escape, that ye may be able to bear it* (1 Corinthians 10:13).

Your temptation is determined by your capacity, but God makes a way of escape. Your victory is determined by your destiny. If you have a great destiny, you will carry a great victory.

What you should do is to protect your destiny by prayer.

Behold, they shall surely gather together, but not by me: whosoever shall gather together against thee shall fall for thy sake (Isaiah 54:13).

Everyone that gathers together against you, your family, health, job, career, business, finances and/or marital life shall perish before your eyes in the name of Jesus Christ. The God of the Hebrews is appearing for you in the name of Jesus Christ.

How do you approach the One who wants to take over your battle?

You approach Him with thanksgiving. You give Him praise with thanksgiving. Moses said in Exodus 15:1 ... *I will sing unto the Lord, for He hath triumphed gloriously: the horse and his rider hath he thrown into the sea.*

Who is like unto thee, O Lord, among the gods? Who is like thee, glorious in holiness, fearful in praises, doing wonders? (Exodus 15:11)

Lift your voice and give God praise and thanks. Lift your voice to heaven and thank the God that has caused you to escape 2014 and to see 2015 up till now. Not everyone who saw yesterday saw today; Thank Him!

Lift your voice to thank Him for your life and destiny and His purpose for you in 2015.

Father, for my star that will shine in 2015 to the maximum, for my destiny, the destiny of my family members and your church, I thank you.

Thank Him one more time for how high He is taking your destiny.

Father, for the maximum you have reserved for me in every good area of my life (business, career, health, family, finance, relationship with you), and for what you have prepared for me, my family and your church I am here to thank you.

Mercy has a lot of effect on a man's destiny. Blind Bartimaeus remained on the way side till mercy met him. When the mercy of Jesus the Son of David met him, mercy did not leave him the same way but relocated him to where he ought to be.

When mercy met Jacob, his story changed. Jacob said, *I am not worthy of the least of all the mercies, and of all the truth, which thou hast shewed unto thy servant; for with my staff I passed over this Jordan; and now I am become two bands* (Genesis 32:10). Without God's mercy you cannot be anything.

Father, release to me the maximum mercy that I, my family, your church and everyone that concerns me needs especially in the month of April in the mighty name of Jesus.

The number four represents the number of Divine intervention, when the God of Israel comes down.

O God of the Hebrews, in this year 2015, especially in the month of April, come down for my favor, come down for my family's favor, come down for your church's favor in the name of Jesus.

Father, arise and cause any warfare that may rise against me, my family, my finance, my health, my destiny and your church in 2015 to perish in the mighty name of Jesus.

Father, remove everything that has drained my faith in 2014. Make my faith stronger; take my faith to maximum this year especially in the month of April in Jesus name.

Decree: **Let every effect of "Egypt" upon my faith, my family, your church, let them perish in the name of Jesus.**

And the Lord said unto Satan, Hast thou considered my servant Job, that there is none like him in the earth, a perfect and an upright man, one that feareth God, and escheweth evil? Then Satan answered the Lord, and said, Doth Job fear God for nought? (Job 1:8-9)

Father, put your edge of protection about me, my family, and your church this year especially in the month of April; and bless the work of my hands in the name of Jesus.

Pray in the Holy Ghost for a minute.

My Prayer for You This Month:

Father we thank you today, for this month of April 2015, in our year of Maximum. Thank you for your love that caused us to escape yesterday, last week, and last month.

Glory be to your wonderful name. Thank you for your colorful destiny planned for us, Thank you for the future you have reserved for us. Take all the praise in the name of Jesus Christ.

Based on what you want to do with our destiny, our destiny and family need your maximum mercy. Release maximum mercy upon us in this 2015 in the name of Jesus Christ. You are the only One who can protect. We commit our destiny, family, lives, and all into your hands. Father, set a hedge around us that Satan cannot penetrate in the name of Jesus Christ.

Take over our battles. Every battle raging over our destiny, Father, take over and give us outstanding victories in the name of Jesus Christ.

As we step into today, let victory songs be heard from us in the name of Jesus Christ. We dedicate April 2015 to you in the name of the Father, the Son, and the Holy Spirit. Amen!

Prayer Charge For April

In the year of maximum, we said turbulence is not under, it is on top. Although cars maybe affected by the blowing of the wind, turbulence affects aircrafts. The reason is not just size. It is because of the space difference. While one is air space the other is land space. If you must go higher, turbulence may appear.

You want God to give you a stronger capacity for any turbulence that will come your way. To say turbulence won't come is an error.

As surely as goodness and mercy will follow you, surely forces against you will gather together. The Bible says that surely they will gather together. It was not a prophet that said that but the Almighty God that said it.

Listen, in your family, in this assembly Satan will not be able to stay in the name of Jesus Christ. Amen.

You want to pray a simple prayer.

Father, every appearance of Satan around me around my family, around your church, in the name of Jesus, we banish them.

After the third temptation in Matthew 4, the Bible says *and Satan departed from him*. He must not stay around you every time. He must leave you alone to enjoy your life. May God make this year a Satan-free year for you in the name of Jesus Christ Amen. Some foods are fat-free. Your life must be Satan-free.

Pray: Father, make 2015 a Satan-free life for me, my family and your church in the name of Jesus.

In Matthew 13: 27, when the man who planted the good seed woke up and his people came to tell him, 'you planted good seed in your farm what happened? He said the enemy has done this. There are lives that are enemy-free, satanic-free; there are some that Satan penetrates.

Job 1:7 says, *and the Lord said unto Satan, Whence comest thou? Then Satan answered the Lord, and said, from going to and fro in the earth, and from walking up and down in it.*

That's why you have to cover yourself, put a hedge around you everywhere so if you meet him on the way it is not trouble for you. That is why the hedge of God must cover you every time.

This year, may God be proud of you. Did you see how proud God was of Job? See how God was flaunting Job's resume. God must be proud of you. He was proud of Jesus. He said this is my beloved son in whom I am well pleased.

Pray: Father, as from today in this year 2015, especially in the month of April, Father help me O Lord that you will be proud of me in the name of Jesus Christ.

Listen, why was God talking to Satan like that? He knew Satan was the accuser of brethren. He has all the records of your wrong. God was saying, challenge what I am saying. May God use the blood to take away all your record that Satan may use against you.

You want to say, **every handwriting written against me that Satan may use against me in the**

year 2015, especially in the month of April, Father, remove them by the blood and nail them to the cross.

If Satan goes anywhere and you can't tell where he is, it means you cannot excuse your hedge any day because you don't know whether you are going where he is. That's why the Bible says that *he that dwelleth in the secret place of the most high shall abide under the shadow of the Almighty*. This is very important.

Read Job 1: 8-10. When Satan tried Job, he found a hedge around him. He said since I cannot get him; let me move forward to his house. If they try you and they don't get you, the next place they try is your house. Now, when he got to his house, he found a hedge. He discovered there was no place in Job's life that was exposed.

You are going to say **Anywhere in my life that is exposed Father, put a hedge around it and whatever area that I might be exposed Lord, knowingly or unknowingly, set your hedge around me.**

In every area of your life that is exposed, may the King of Glory cover you in the name of Jesus Christ. Some people are exposed to cancer unknowingly. Some people are exposed to evil without knowing. Some people are exposed to one calamity or the other, and they don't know.

Look at what David said in Psalm 140:7 *O God the Lord, the strength of my salvation, thou hast covered my head in the day of battle.*

You can't go uncovered in the day of battle. You are going to say **Father, in any day of battle in the year 2015, especially in the month of April 2015 cover my head, the head of my family and your church.** Your head is covered in the name of Jesus Christ. Your finances are covered in the name of Jesus Christ. Your career, job and business are covered in the name of Jesus Christ. Your future, marriage, your home is covered in the name of Jesus Christ.

You need to be covered. God set a hedge around Job and around his household. He had a hedge around on every side. You need to understand scriptures; because you are covered does not mean you should relax. If they don't get you, they will look for somebody else to get in your family. Can I ask you a question? When they didn't get Job who did they kill? His children.

It is warfare and you must be ready to fight also. Fight the good fight of faith.

The number four is the number of secret solutions. In 2 Kings 7:1-9, they had invaded the city, plundered everything and everywhere was dry. The four lepers said if they stayed there they would die, if they went they might be killed. But they saw a solution that others were not seeing. While others were lavishing in famine, they entered breakthrough and surplus. In the time of famine, God will show you solution that will bring surplus in the name of Jesus Christ.

As a matter of fact, when they had taken and eaten to their satisfaction, they said, we are not doing the right thing. Let us go and invite other people to come enjoy. You will have so much in 2015, you will call others to come and enjoy with you in the name of Jesus Christ. Listen the only reason the wise virgins were stingy was because they didn't have enough. They were wise, they were virgins but they were poor. Don't combine poverty with spiritual virtue. It spoils your testimony and your integrity. You can't be stingy. The Bible says it is more blessed to give than to receive. They refused to give because they didn't have enough.

Father, in 2015 especially in the fourth month, the month of April, in our year of maximum, show us the secret solution that will lead to wealth in the name of Jesus.

There are four cardinals direction of the earth, the North, South, East and the West. You want to address the entire cardinal points of the earth.

North favor me, South favor me, East favor me, West favor me. Every cardinal point I turn to in this year 2015, must favor me.

Lord, your people are grateful. We are thankful for the confidence you have put in us, for the future ahead of us. How will Satan rob us again, seeing all you have put in place for our maximum? That is why we give you alone the glory, honor, the adoration and the power. King of glory, King of the earth, we thank you. The One that called the year 2015, the year of Maximum, whose mighty touch turned the bread to His body, who turned the wine to His blood, we give you praise and thanks in the name of the Father, in the name of the Son and in the name of the Holy Spirit.

Father, we thank you for April 2015 is settled already. There's someone reading this devotional, the Lord says to tell you that you should have been exposed to a terminal disease but because you have asked him to cover you, He said "I have covered you permanently". Father, we ask one thing, we want you to be proud of us. Help us to do things that will make you proud of us in the name of Jesus Christ. Glory and honor be to your name O Lord, in Jesus name we pray.

Chapter Five
May 2015

Welcome into the presence of the Ancient of Days, the God of all living and moving things. *For in him we live, and move, and have our being; as certain also of your own poets have said, For we are also his offspring* (Acts 17:28).

Not every living person can move, some have to be moved. The man at the gate called Beautiful was living but could not move. The Bible says he was *laid daily at the gate of the temple which is called Beautiful.* One day the one who could not move began to move. Today becomes your day to begin to move in the name of Jesus Christ.

'Thou hast granted me life and favor, and thy visitation hath preserved my spirit (Job 10:12). The ability to live was granted to you and I by the Almighty God. Only God can do this, He does not have any co-performers. This is why the Bible says *this is the Lord's doing, and it is marvelous in our eyes* (Matthew 21:42).

May this month be filled with only what God can do. May God decorate your entire year with what only He can do in the name of Jesus Christ.

From his mother's womb, they found he was living but at birth, they found he was not moving. What has "stopped moving" in your life? What is that thing that is no longer advancing in your life? When things stop moving, it is a sign that there is no progress. God has a commitment not just to make you live, but to make you move.

Whatever has stopped moving, in whatever area in your life you cannot see a significant sign of progress; this month of May is ushering you into a life of amazing progress in the name of Jesus Christ, Amen!

Having your being means retaining your sanity. Nebuchadnezzar at some point was living and moving but didn't have his being. Instead of being a human being, he was an animal being. You must understand that to live a complete life only comes from Him. It is important to know where we are starting from today. The more you know how to depend on Him, the more He will take you to your maximum.

Nebuchadnezzar thought he was responsible for his greatness, and God withdrew his being; making him half man and half animal.

May God take whatever may cause you to lose your being from your life in the name of Jesus Christ.

The more you know how to depend on Him the more He will take you to your maximum. *Trust in the LORD with all thine heart; and lean not unto thine own understanding. In all thy ways acknowledge him, and he shall direct thy paths* (Proverbs 3:5-6).

In ***all*** your ways acknowledge Him. Let Him know He is Lord over your heart, your all in all. Let Him know that without Him nothing exists. Give Him the glory.

David said in Psalm 146:2, *While I live will I praise the LORD: I will sing praises unto my God while I have any being.*

Moving is very important to us today because in Genesis 1 we find the amazing description of creational work.

And God said, Let the waters bring forth abundantly the moving creature that hath life, and fowl that may fly above the earth in the open firmament of heaven (Genesis 1:20)

Everything made to this point could not move, and could not produce after its kind or multiply. On the fifth day a new dimension of creation appeared.

May God use this fifth month to give a new dimension and direction to your life and destiny in Jesus name.

May God make this fifth month become your month of divine production in the name of Jesus Christ.

I decree concerning your life: May the month of May usher into your life and family a new movement in the name of Jesus.

It takes movement to leave minimum to maximum. As you fill up your gas tank you see the gauge move from empty to full, just like that your life must move from minimum to maximum today in the name of Jesus Christ. Every work of your hands is leaving minimum and going to maximum in the name of Jesus. You need the miracle of ***movement*** to move from your current level to maximum. Your businesses, marriage, finance need the miracle of movement.

The man at the pool of Bethesda was at the same point for thirty-eight years, unable to move. He reported that when the angel came to trouble the water, others got there before him. Life cheats you when you don't move. I decree to you in the name of Jesus Christ: whatever needs to move for you this year will move in the name of Jesus Christ.

As Abram, he needed movement to become Abraham. God asked him to move, leave his kindred and his father's house.

If Jesus didn't move in John 11 when they called him to heal Lazarus; Lazarus would have not been raised from the dead. Jesus will move to intervene in your case in the name of Jesus Christ.

In Genesis 1:20 nothing was described as abundant until the fifth day. May God grant you abundance that you have never seen before in Jesus name.

On the fifth day, birds were created. The fifth day is the day of high fliers. High fliers are those on top of everything. They are never below, always on top. In the name of Jesus of Nazareth, in this fifth month of 2015, your life and destiny will fly higher. Also, the birds were to fly in the open firmament of Heaven. This indicates that they had enough room to fly. Thus the fifth day is the day when God creates room for His people.

I decree in the name of Jesus: In this fifth month of 2015, God will make room for you.

In Geneis 26, Isaac said *Rehoboth, for the Lord has blessed us and has made room for us.* In 2015, you must enjoy the blessing of God making room for you.

Lift your voice and bless the One that has kept you alive to see this month.

Thank Him for all the blessings of the fifth day, the blessings of movement, of advancement (in work, business, career, health, opportunity, blessings, ministry, and every good area of life), and the blessing of being a high flier that you are going to enjoy.

Father, for every blessing you are going to decorate my life with in this fifth month, I am here to thank you on behalf of myself, my family, and your church in Jesus name.

He was first Simon and became Peter, Abram became Abraham, Sarai became Sarah and Hosea became Joshua. These name changes (as seen in scripture) represent movement. In every Simon there is a Peter. In every Abram is an Abraham. In every Sarai is a Sarah. Lift your voice and thank Him.

For every movement my destiny will enjoy in becoming a new me in this fifth month of 2015, I give you praise and thanks.

There is something that must move with you in this 2015: His mercy. David said in Psalm 23:6, *goodness and mercy shall follow me*. If goodness and mercy is not moving, they cannot follow you. If His mercy does not move with you, you are in trouble.

Father, let there be movement of mercy towards me, my family, and your church this year, especially this month of May in Jesus name.

Blind Bartimaeus couldn't move, mercy moved towards him. He couldn't enjoy movement but mercy came to him where he was. Wherever you are, may the mercy of God move towards you and all yours in the name of Jesus Christ.

I decree one more time, may the mercy of God move towards you and all that concerns you in the name of Jesus Christ.

And God said, Let the waters bring forth abundantly the moving creature that hath life, and fowl that may fly above the earth in the open firmament of heaven (Genesis 1:20)

When a friend wants to introduce you to another friend, they will say, "Meet Mr./Ms.". In the same way, may God introduce you to abundance in this fifth month. It is possible not to find abundance even though it is there. Peter did not find fish even though it was there in abundance.

Father, in this year of 2015 and especially in the month of May introduce abundance into my life in the name of Jesus.

I prophesy: There is someone praying these prayers. Your net was empty in 2014 but God will introduce you to a net breaking breakthrough in the name of Jesus Christ.

God created every moving creature in abundance.

Father, this year and especially this month of May introduce a new dimension of abundance into my life and family in the name of Jesus.

Any area of my life that has not moved and not advanced enough, Father take away limitations from me. Advancement and movement that only comes from you that I could never imagine; grant unto me, my family and your church in Jesus name.

Pray in the Holy Ghost for a minute. Give Him thanks.

My Prayer for You This Month:

Ancient of Days we bless your name again and again, seeing what you have done again this month. Giving us a divine feeling on what the entire year will look like. Thank you because by your truth, we can discern what you want to do, because you will do the things you have said.

Thank you for opening our understanding to the trend of the fifth day. Glory be to you in the name of Jesus Christ. Thank you that in you we live, we move and have our being. Blessed be your wonderful name, in the name of Jesus Christ.

Thank you because of mercy that will be moving towards our direction. Thank you for granting mercy that will move towards us. You said great is thy mercy towards me. Be glorified O God, in the name of Jesus Christ.

When Jabez prayed, you granted his requests. As your people have prayed, everything they have requested, grant in the name of Jesus Christ. Blessed be your glorious name O Lord. We dedicate the month of May and the rest of year to you in the name of the Father, the Son and the Holy Spirit. Thank you Father Lord, in Jesus precious name we pray, Amen!

Prayer Charge For May:

They looked unto Him, they were lightened and their faces were not ashamed. As you look unto Him in this fifth month and throughout your year 2015, you will not find shame in the name of Jesus Christ. They looked unto Him. There is somebody we look to whose face eliminates shame. People met Him with shame but He removed their shame. Whatever may be the shame you are dealing with, battling with, publicly or privately, silently or loudly, visible or invisible may God remove it in the name of Jesus Christ.

I remember the testimony of a lady who was still bed wetting at the age of 25, before God delivered her. She was unable to accept a marriage proposal from any man, because of her bed wetting situation. This was a private shame, but the Lord of Heaven, took away her shame in just one day. Whatever shame is associated with your destiny, the One you are looking up to will remove your shame in the name of Jesus Christ.

I will lift up mine eyes unto the hills, from whence cometh my help. My help cometh from the Lord, which made heaven and the earth (Psalm 121:1-2). The same God that made the Heaven and the Earth sent me to you. Whatever shame you have battled with, whether personally or over a loved one, where the case of a loved one is shameful to the family, the Lord asked me to tell you He is taking away your shame in the name of Jesus Christ.

God asked me to tell someone, this year He will give you answers of comfort in the name of Jesus Christ. He said announce to a destiny, they are receiving comfortable answers in the name of Jesus Christ.

Lets take another look at the trend of the fifth day. Until the fifth day, nothing multiplied, nothing moved, nothing flew in the air. You want to command the blessing of the fifth day upon your life. From Genesis 1:20, I can list 50 blessings of the fifth day. The fifty I will list to you is too small compared with what God wants to do. So you will summarize and say: **Every blessing and trend of the fifth day let it be seen in my life.** Some of you will fly to some heights in life and ask yourself, if I knew life was this sweet I would have been serving Jesus a long time ago. So life can be this sweet and colorful? You will be begging God to forgive you for not serving Him since you were in the womb.

Some of you will enter some open doors that you will say, "I heard this happen to others, I didn't know it was going to happen to me".

In some peoples' case their foundation is not good enough for maximum. What determines the height of a building is its foundation, and some foundations need to be repaired. May God repair whatever is in your foundation that is not strong enough to carry you to the height He wants to take you in Jesus name.

We wanted to upgrade our altar, and I found some designs, took pictures of it, and sent the pictures to the architect. The architect said he was unable to confirm if we could make those changes without knowing the weight of all the materials in the picture. He indicated that knowing the weight, would help him confirm if the foundation of the building would sustain the upgrade. I asked if the weight would not sustain it, what our options would be? He responded, "either we use lighter materials or we strengthen the foundation." "How do we strengthen the foundation?" I asked. By pulling down the building, he responded. Which obviously was not a valid option. What man is unable to do, God can do it. Whatever is in your foundation that won't allow you to climb to your maximum, our God can fix it in the name of Jesus Christ.

Let me explain this to you. Some things are affecting some of us because they were done in the early days of our lives. Those things have tainted our lives. Some things have happened, nobody may know but somehow they have influenced your life today. When you trace your calamities, some things at the beginning went wrong. That is why Jesus himself said, from the beginning it was not so. Whatever went wrong, the hand of your Savior can fix it, I therefore decree that the hand of Jesus will go to your foundation and fix it right now in the name of Jesus Christ.

For example, when a child grows up in a violent environment, anger becomes a part of their life and that anger can prevent them from entering heights. Anger denied Moses from entering where God wanted to take him. God said he should speak to the rock, but in anger he struck the rock twice. He thought he was hitting the rock, he did not know he was hitting the Rock of Ages. 1 Corinthians 10:1-4 says Moreover, *brethren, I would not that ye should be ignorant, how that all our fathers were under the cloud, and all passed through the sea; And were all baptized unto Moses in the cloud and in the sea; And did all eat the same spiritual meat; And did all drink the same spiritual drink: for they drank of that spiritual Rock that followed them: and that Rock was Christ.* Given this, God said, my intention for you was to enter into the promise land but for what you have done I will limit your maximum. His foundation affected him. That is why I want you pray that whatever has gone wrong at your beginning that might prevent you from getting to where you are going, Father fix that problem.

What people resort to doing is to give you medication to solve all kinds of problems. The truth is no matter the amount of medication you are taking, it cannot fix your destiny. It might slow you down, reduce the speed of your pace so you are not active but it will not solve your problem. However, the One who created you can fix your problem. The manufacturer of a product can fix the product's problem. That is why we run to the One that made us. The Bible calls Him the Maker of Heaven and earth.

Pray: Father, whatever has gone wrong in my foundation, knowingly and unknowingly, the ones I can remember and those I cannot, O Lord, arise, fix my foundation.

Our foundation has affected some of us; we have made wrong decisions in life that we have been unable to un-make or recover from. The Repairer of the Breach (Isaiah 58:12) has sent me to tell you that He wants to repair what is broken.

Remember the story of the woman who ran to Solomon, to tell him that she and her friend had agreed to eat their sons. She said, while they were sleeping the friend had exchanged the babies, do you remember that story? If the child was exchanged and the mother did not cry out for her child, someone else would have been his mother without his knowledge because there was no DNA in those days. Many things have happened in our lives without our knowledge, which is why you are going to tell God, what I don't know that may have gone wrong, stretch down your hands to my life and fix my life.

Lord, today, we want to make sure that all things are ready for our maximum. You said tell the owner, the good master that all things are ready. So things have to be a particular way. Therefore, concerning the lives of these ones reading this devotional, whatever is no longer so, that has gone wrong and the hands of man cannot fix, please fix because you are the only One who can fix it in Jesus mighty name.

You said for we are not the one that made ourselves. It is you who made us; and since you made us, we are your people and the sheep of your pasture. Then we have no problem, because a maker can fix whatever is bad in his products. We are your products; out of mercy fix us in the name of Jesus Christ.

What other service companies have tried and can't fix is mailed back to the manufacturer. O King of glory, our life warranty is with you. Whatever has gone bad concerning our lives; fix them in the name of Jesus Christ, fix them to their very foundation in the name of Jesus Christ.

Whatever powers wants to hold your foundation ransom, may the consuming fire appear and consume them in the name of Jesus Christ. Whatever powers signed an eternal covenant with them that they won't let you go, today by the Blood of Jesus, we destroy their hold in the name of Jesus Christ. You are free today in the name of Jesus. May your rest of your life henceforth be dependent upon the covenant of the Blood of Jesus and may the Blood of Jesus become your foundation. So shall it be. We sanctify your roots, your foundation by the Blood of Jesus in the name of the Father, in the name of the Son and in the name of the Holy Spirit. Glory be to God.

Chapter Six
June 2015

Welcome into the presence of God and into the sixth month of this year.

The word of God says *No man can come to me, except the Father which hath sent me draw him: and I will raise him up at the last day* (John 6.44). If He does not draw you, you cannot come to Him, He has to draw you for you to come. It becomes a privilege, anytime you find yourself coming to the Lord to know that there is somebody working in you *both to will and do of his good pleasure* (Philippians 2:13).

It is God working in you, both to will and to do of His good pleasure not your alarm clock. We must understand this so that we can give Him thanks very well for everything He is working out in us. He just does not work things out for you He also works things out in you. There is a dimension of His working out for you and there is a dimension of His working in you. Scripture says according in Romans 8:26, *Likewise the Spirit also helpeth our infirmities: for we know not what we should pray for as we ought: but the Spirit itself maketh intercession for us with groanings which cannot be uttered.*

When it comes to the issue of prayer, your reliance and dependency on the Holy Spirit is very crucial to the effectiveness of your prayer life. The more you rely and depend on Him, the more He helps you. He can help and assist you in your infirmity so that when you are weak you can say you are strong according to 2 Corinthians 12:10b.

His word says let the weak say I am strong because His strength is made perfect in weaknesses. Moses was on the mountain for 40 days, and the Lord gave him grace. When he went to the mountain he was more than 80 years old. We saw that strange things happened to him, because he learnt how to depend and rely on God. When he returned from the mountain the Bible says his face began to shine with the glory of God.

Every glory your life has missed before, from now on your life will reflect those glories in the name of Jesus Christ.

There are glories you don't find at the bottom of the mountain, you find them at the top of the mountain. If Moses did not go to the mountain that glory will not be revealed in him. There are locations for glory, prayer and fasting is a location for glory. Certain things will not become your experience until you climb the mountain. For example, in Obadiah 1:17, the Bible says, *But upon mount Zion shall be deliverance, and there shall be holiness; and the house of Jacob shall possess their possessions.* He said 'upon' mount Zion so if you stay and remain at the bottom you are wasting your time. Climb the mountain. Until they were on the Mountain of Transfiguration certain things did not happen to the disciples. You have come to the top of mountain today and you will not go back the way you have come in the name of Jesus Christ.

Climbing the mountain, waiting upon the Lord, is your greatest advantage to enjoying a life that is different from a former experience.

When Moses went to that mountain the Bible says Joshua was at the bottom of the mountain waiting for him but his face didn't shine. It was Moses who was at the top of the mountain that had a shining face.

For your destiny and life to shine, you must climb on the mountain.

Certain things only happen when you are on the mountain. Jesus and some disciples were on the mountain and suddenly Jesus was transfigured before them. This did not happen while they were at the bottom of the mountain. Matthew 17:1-2 says, *And after six days Jesus taketh Peter, James, and John his brother, and bringeth them up into an high mountain apart, And was transfigured before them: and his face did shine as the sun, and his raiment was white as the light.* Some experiences are only acquirable on the mountain; so do not take waiting upon the Lord for granted.

Moses was unaware of his shining face, Exodus 34:29b says, '*that Moses wist not that the skin of his face shone while he talked with him*'. Something happen to you on the mountain that you are not aware of until you step down from the mountain. Many things are going on already in your life as you are praying, many things are entering your spirit man, and many things are entering your future and destiny that you are not even aware of.

In the year 2015, your life will shine in the name of Jesus Christ, Amen!

Others will keep wondering why your case is different and things are easy for you. They won't know you have done something uneasy to stay on the mountain for this long. No act of spiritual endeavor goes unrewarded.

When Moses came to God, he had his portion for him for the 40 days. This portion was the guide, which is called the tablet or His commandments for His people. He delivered the provision that would guide the life of Israel to Moses.

On this mountain, God will put things in your life that will be benefit other people in the name of Jesus Christ. God will deliver things into your life that other people will benefit from. Imagine if Moses did not stay on the mountain, we won't have the Ten Commandments today.

God is still looking for people who come to the mountain to pray and receive from Heaven. He needs people who He can depend on, without these people the earth will experience spiritual famine. He sends solutions to the earth through these people who come to the mountain.

To the poor, God is sending prosperity through you. To the homeless, He is sending help through you. To nations, He is sending wisdom through you. The solutions to the earth are sent through people who come to the mountain. You have come to the mountain; God will make you a solution in the name of Jesus Christ, Amen!

Whenever you come to the mountain, you come to a place where Heaven makes you a solution. God is always giving things to people who come to the mountain.

As you have come, you will not be allowed to go back empty in the name of Jesus Christ, Amen!

We will consider a few things about the sixth day trend for the sixth month of June, and then we will begin to thank God.

It is to good to understand how God works. Moses knew His ways, but the children of Israel knew His acts.

When you know His ways, you will create waves on the earth. You become an amazement to people.

Let us look at the working of God on the sixth day. Many of us have limited the work of the sixth day to just the creation of man but that is not how the sixth day started.

And God said, Let the earth bring forth the living creature after his kind, cattle, and creeping thing, and beast of the earth after his kind: and it was so. And God made the beast of the earth after his kind, and cattle after their kind, and everything that creepeth upon the earth after his kind: and God saw that it was good. And God said, Let us make man in our image, after our likeness: and let them have dominion over the fish of the sea, and over the fowl of the air, and over the cattle, and over all the earth, and over every creeping thing that creepeth upon the earth (Genesis 1:24-26)

Before man was made on the sixth day, God created another species of creation called animals. On the fifth day, His vision was to create animals that multiply in the waters and fly in the air. On the sixth day, He began to create what moves on the earth and created the cattle, beasts and creeping animals. He could have created man like those animals but decided to create man differently.

Things may happen to others, but may God make the month of June a different experience for you in the name of Jesus Christ, Amen!

May the power of difference come upon your destiny this year especially in the month of June in the name of Jesus Christ.

Others may suffer, perish, be stranded, hungry, not favored, but your case is different in the name of Jesus Christ. In this sixth month, may the power of difference work to your advantage in the name of Jesus Christ.

God intended man to be different. God's first favor to man was to make us different.

Say to yourself: "I am different."

No matter what the experiences of others are, yours will be different.

Secondly, everything God created before man was to provide for him. The sixth day is the number of provision. He made sure nothing was missing before you appeared.

God will put back anything missing from your life, family and His church in the name of Jesus.

Again, Genesis 1:26 says, *God said, "let us make man in our image.* This is the first time the word ***our*** shows up in the scriptures, implying that for the first time, the combined effort of Heaven came together for one creation.

In this sixth month, may all the resources of Heaven come together for your favor in the name of Jesus Christ.

"Let us make man". Every other thing was spoken into being, only man was made.

The power of the creation of man happened on the sixth day, because of the order of the sixth month, something amazing will happen through your hands in the name of Jesus Christ, Amen!

When God makes you, no one can un-make you. May God make nations, your generation and your contemporaries envy you in the name of Jesus Christ.

God still wants people to show up in places and radiate His likeness, so people will say: God has shown up here even though it was a man who came. When they saw what Paul had done, they said, *The gods are come to us in the likeness of men* because the things that happened through Paul were things that only comes from God.

May God make you to be like Him in all areas of life in the name of Jesus Christ.

It is not a coincidence that man was made on the sixth day and when the word was to become man in the announcement about the birth of Jesus, it occurred on the sixth month.

Luke 1.26-31, *And in the sixth month the angel Gabriel was sent from God unto a city of Galilee, named Nazareth. To a virgin espoused to a man whose name was Joseph, of the house of David; and the virgin's name was Mary. And the angel came in unto her, and said, Hail, thou that art highly favored, the Lord is with thee: blessed art thou among women. And when she saw him, she was troubled at his saying, and cast in her mind what manner of salutation this should be. And the angel said unto her, Fear not, Mary: for thou hast found favor with God. And, behold, thou shalt conceive in thy womb, and bring forth a son, and shalt call his name JESUS* (Luke 1:26-31).

There are many inventions and world wonders that the world is yet to see, because of the order of the sixth day, may God put in your hands those miracles and wonder ideas and innovations in the name of Jesus.

The difference that appeared on the sixth day was the difference of favor. Favor is the greatest possession that you need on the earth. When you are favored, everything lines up for you. The angel announced to the woman on the sixth day, *Thou that art highly favored ...blessed art thou among women*.

May the favor you have never tasted, seen or experienced before locate you in the name of Jesus.

Your first response should be that of thanksgiving.

Father, for allowing me to see this day in the sixth month of this year, my year of Maximum, I am here to say thank you.

Father, for including me, my family and your church in your plan and agenda for this year, I am here praise you and to say thank you.

God has special things He wants to do in 2015 and He wants to include you in those special things.

Father, thank you for including me, my family and your church in the special things you want to do this year.

When God wants to do something special, He looks for people to include. When God wanted to save man, He chose to include Mary in His agenda. May God select you to be a part of His plans for 2015 in the name of Jesus Christ.

There is power in mercy, but there is a secret to converting mercy to favor. One reason Mary was involved in the salvation plan and agenda, was that she found favor.

May God cause you to find favor in the name of Jesus Christ, Amen!

I decree you will not just find and locate favor but favor will find and locate you in the name of Jesus Christ, Amen!

Thou shalt arise, and have mercy upon Zion: for the time to favor her, yea, the set time, is come (Psalm 102:13).

Without God rising for you in mercy, you cannot find favor so without mercy you cannot receive favor.

Father, this year arise for me and show me favor in the name of Jesus.

Favor qualified Mary to play a strategic role in the salvation agenda and placed her there.

Father, this year especially in the month of June, let your favor be a difference maker for me, my family and your church in the name of Jesus.

God will do wonders this year but to qualify for it and be an active player, you will need the favor of God as it was the favor of God that qualified Mary.

Father, this year may your favor qualify me, my family and your church in the name of Jesus.

In Genesis 1, the Bible says, and *God said let us make man* so everything He said He did. He made man in His image.

Father, everything you have said, everything you have spoken concerning my 2015, and this month June, let them come to pass in the name of Jesus.

In Genesis 21:1, the Bible says, *and the lord visited Sarah as he had said and the Lord did unto Sarah as he had spoken.* He did exactly what He said and what He spoke.

Father, this year, especially this month of June, visit me O lord as you have said, do unto me as you have spoken.

My Prayer for You This Month:

Our Father in Heaven, we thank you exceedingly for the power of life that is absolutely under your control. Satan wanted to kill Job but you said he shouldn't touch his life and he couldn't touch it. The greatest enemy of the soul of man couldn't touch him because you said so. We know we are alive today because you said so and we know we will be alive through this year because you said so. Take all the praise and glory in the name of Jesus Christ.

We have seen the beauty of your trend of the sixth day. May the mercy that causes a man to enjoy all of God become our portion in the name of Jesus Christ.

No doubt Heaven will still be doing special things this year, especially this month of June. O King of Glory, may mercy and your favor qualify us to be a player in the name of Jesus Christ.

In a very special way, you involved a woman, a young girl, in the salvation agenda, the greatest agenda of mankind. Let your favor qualify us to be players in your 2015 agenda on the earth.

The power of difference was released on the sixth day. As from today, may our life become different in the name of Jesus Christ.

Things that are different stand out and are outstanding. As from today, may we begin to stand out and live outstanding lives in the name of Jesus Christ.

We dedicate the entire month of June to you, in the name of the Father, the Son and the Holy Spirit. Thank you Holy Father, in Jesus wonderful name we pray, Amen!!

Prayer Charge For June

In Genesis 1:25, we see that God made the beast of the earth after his kind and cattle after their kind and everything that creepeth upon the earth after his kind. And God saw that it was good.

If you look at the fifth day work, God did not assess the fifth day work as good. *And God blessed them, saying, Be fruitful, and multiply, and fill the waters in the seas, and let fowl multiply in the earth. And the evening and the morning were the fifth day* (Genesis 1:22-23).

God suspended His assessment until the sixth day. Whatever was missing before in your life, the trend of the sixth day requires their replacement.

Whatever is missing in my 2015, on the platform of the prophetic order of the sixth day, Father, put it in my life.

Father, whatever has been missing in my life, in my destiny, in my family O God in this sixth month, put them there, put back my missing pieces in the name of Jesus.

In verse 26-28, the Bible says, *let us make man in our image after our likeness and let them have dominion*. This implies that you are not permitted to be dominated. You are the one to dominate. Say, 'I will dominate'. Whatever is dominating you is in the wrong order, you are supposed to be the dominant factor, dominant species. You are not the prey or victim in life.

Father, whatever has dominated me before in the name of Jesus, let there be a reversal, I will dominate in every area of life in the name of Jesus.

Father, this year, especially in this month of June I will dominate financially in the name of Jesus. Father, give me financial dominion.

Father, this year, the power, the ability, the grace to be rich towards you, give unto me O Lord, give unto my family, your church in the name of Jesus.

My wife shared with me a story about a patient that was in the hospital to have her baby. The woman requested the use a Jacuzzi, but the hospital didn't have any. This woman decided to pay for the installation of several Jacuzzis in the birthing center, to help other patients that come to have their babies. It's not her hospital, but she donated millions of dollars to the hospital. She was rich towards the hospital and towards man. You have to be rich towards God.

You must have a heart for the kingdom of God and to develop people. If you cannot part with $1, you won't part with $100. Now if you've never parted with $100, and you ask God to bless you and promise that you'll part with $12,000, God will say you are a liar. He will check your history, and know that you cannot make good on that promise. God has to give us the ability to be rich towards Him.

One day, a person was holding a sign by the roadside at the airport and asking for money and I had $20, $5 and $1 bills. God asked me to give him the $20 bill, but I tried to make the argument that the guy would probably buy something to smoke with it. God told me to let him do whatever he wants with it, and reminded me it is more blessed to give. After I gave the person, the $20 bill, he said God bless you, this is the highest amount I have ever been given. The man I was accusing and judging just by looking at him was simply looking for money to eat. I judged him because stinginess did not want me to give to him. I was judging his condition and God said give him; it is none of your business. Glory be to God. Ask God to enlarge your heart in giving.

Let's touch on the mystery of the stars. In Genesis 1, the Bible describes the creation and role of the sun, moon and stars including what they stand for. Genesis 1:14 says, *And God said, Let there be lights in the firmament of the heaven to divide the day from the night; and let them be for signs, and for seasons, and for days, and years".* This includes every light in the firmament: sun, moon and stars. Which implies that each of these elements in the firmament represents or stands for day and night. They also stand for a sign.

When Jesus was born, the wise men saw a star. One said for we have seen a star, a sign. The sign they saw was a star, because each star in Heaven is also meant for signs not just to give light.

May God make your year a sign to the world in the name of Jesus Christ. The stars are not only for signs; they also represent seasons and days. If they can represent days, it means they can represent weeks, months and years. Since they are for signs and days, a star can represent your month. The astrologers say you have a star and even have names for the stars because they are operating from the principle of the scripture.

When Joseph had his dream he saw 12 stars and the moon and the sun. His father said, do you mean that I and your mother and your brothers will bow to you? It means the father Jacob was the sun, the mother the moon, and the brothers were the stars. There were 12 sons of Jacob and he saw 12 stars, each of his brothers represented stars. This means the first son is a star, and since we have established that stars can represent night and days, weeks, month and years, you can call Reuben your January.

What is the star of the sixth day? The star of the sixth day is the man called Isaachar. Who is Isaachar? Isaachar is a man with understanding of times and seasons and knowing what Israel ought to do. Let me say this to you, the secret to success is knowing what to do. When the disciples didn't know what to do, Jesus knew what to do, see John 6.

The secret of lifting and to be outstanding in life is knowing what to do. Nebuchadnezzar was going to kill everybody but Daniel knew what to do. He said to the King I will tell you your dream and the interpretation. By knowing what to do people who were supposed to die, escaped. The sixth month is the month of understanding. You are going to say, in every area of my life, baptize me with understanding that my peers do not have.

Pray in the Holy Ghost.

When you were born, your star also appeared. The Bible says, in Him we found the spirit of wisdom and counsel. Solomon dominated his generation through the power of wisdom and understanding. Daniel dominated in a strange land. The people even said he had the understanding of the gods. Understanding makes a man outstanding.

If there is a blessing after the order of the sixth day that we need, it is the blessing of understanding. Among all God has given to us, He said with all thy getting, get understanding. Understanding delivers a man from mediocrity, puts him on the platform of prominence.

In the year of maximum, especially in the sixth month may the strange grace of strange understanding be yours. They said to Daniel, only the gods know what you know. This is understanding that is beyond human level. In our careers, in our businesses, in the areas of our endeavors, O King of glory, baptize us with it in the name of Jesus Christ. The scripture says, the wisdom of the godhead dwells in you, you are wisdom embodied. Blessed be your name Jesus.

May the glory of your star surpass that of your peers in the name of Jesus Christ. And wherever darkness dominated, because of the light coming out of you, that environment will be changed in the name of Jesus Christ. I decree you will become a world changer in the name of Jesus Christ.

Chapter Seven
July 2015

Hallelujah! We welcome everyone again into the presence of the One whose words matter concerning a man's destiny. To the presence of the One whose word is the final say. Anyone can speak, anyone can do anything but the word of the Lord our God is final. It does not matter what anyone has said or when it was said, what matters is what the Almighty God has said. In the matter of a man's destiny, His word is what matters. That is why when the earth was without form and void and He said let there be light, darkness had no argument to what He had said. In all issues of life, in every environment everyone defers to the one whose word matters the most.

When darkness appeared at the beginning of creation the earth was without form and void because God had not said anything.

Darkness was everywhere.

Emptiness was everywhere because God had not spoken. The moment God said let there be light, the story changed.

Before He spoke, everything continued the way they were. You have to understand the power and authority of the Almighty, the Ancient of Days. Genesis 1:1-2 says, *In the beginning God created the heaven and the earth. And the earth was without form, and void; and darkness was upon the face of the deep. And the Spirit of God moved upon the face of the waters.*

Darkness dominated and continued because God had said nothing. That is why it is dangerous for God not to say anything about your future and life. As long as God is quiet or silent everything continues as it is. John 8:4-9, tells the story of the woman caught the woman in the very act of adultery, her accusers kept speaking until Jesus said *He who is without sin among you, let him be the first to throw a stone at her.* And when He looked up everybody had disappeared.

Accusers, enemies continue until He speaks on your case. Genesis 1:3, *'let there be light'.* As soon as His word came darkness had to vamoose because God had said something.

This year, may Heaven not be silent over your case, matter and issue in the name of Jesus Christ.

Whatever has hindered you, whatever has dominated your life before, because God has spoken concerning your 2015, they are giving way in the name of Jesus Christ.

The man in John 5, by the pool of Bethesda had the infirmity for thirty-eighty years, until Jesus spoke on over his case. Unless the One that has the final say is involved, your life will continue the way it is. It does not matter what effort you are making, Satan has the power to frustrate every effort.

Mark 5:25-34, tells us about the woman with the issue of blood who had spent all she had in search for healing. She had suffered in the hands of physicians, but her situation was getting worse, because the Ancient of Days was not involved. The minute He got involved it was like the infirmity never existed.

Today we are going to pray for the involvement of the Ancient of Days in this month, and for the rest of the year. Every issue of blood in your life ceases now in the name of Jesus Christ.

John 9:1-2, *And as Jesus passed by, he saw a mam which was blind from his birth. And his disciples asked him, "Rabbi who sinned, this man or his parents, that he would be born blind?* Conversation and stories continue in your life until God gets involved. When the word of the King appeared, the darkness that had dominated him disappeared.

Because of the involvement of the Ancient of Days, every evil is disappearing from your life in Jesus Name.

Sarah continued in barrenness until God spoke on her case. According to Genesis 18:9-13, she remained a barren woman until God said to Abraham where is your wife? God told her husband she will have a son and she began to laugh. And God heard the woman laugh but she did not know the One who spoke had the final say.

You might be saying 'I have heard that before', 'somebody has said that before', it does not matter who/what has said what, when the Ancient of Days says it, it will come to pass. He is not a man that He will lie nor the son of man that He will repent. If He has spoken it, it will come to pass. Not a jot of His word will return to Him void (Matthew 5:18). Forever O God, thy word is settled in heaven.

God visited Sarah and spoke to her in chapter 18. He did unto her in chapter 21 as He had said. In this year 2015, everything God has said concerning you, you will see them come to pass in Jesus Name.

Everything your ears have heard concerning your 2015, concerning your life, family, future, career, business you will see them coming to pass in the name of Jesus.

The Bible says regarding the woman called Elizabeth, that she would have a child. Everybody had given her a name 'barren', but the name God gave her: 'mother of John' was the most important.

Whatever name the world, the doctors have given you does not matter. The name God has given you is what matters. The bible says, *at the name of Jesus every knee should bow, of things in heaven, and things in earth, and things under the earth; and that every tongue should confess that Jesus Christ is Lord, to the glory of God the Father* (Philippians 2:10-11).

When God spoke concerning her case, the world that called her barren became disappointed. They gathered with her later to celebrate what God had done for her.

In 2015, especially in the 7th month, men will gather concerning your matter to celebrate with you in Jesus Name.

How does God get involved? God gets involved through His word. God did not say anything for four hundred years between the book of Malachi and Matthew; He ignored creation during that time. Four hundred years passed, until God showed mercy and spoke concerning creation.

I decree over the matters of your life; May God show mercy in the name of Jesus Christ.

After four hundred years, God decided to get involved by sending His son. John 1:1 says, *In the beginning was the Word, and the Word was with God, and the Word was God.* John 1:14, *And the Word was made flesh, and dwelt among us, (and we beheld his glory, the glory as of the only begotten of the Father,) full of grace and truth.*

God gets involved through the instrument and person of His word. When His word goes forth concerning your case everything must submit to what God has said. The moment the word came to the earth everything obeyed Him. Even the wind and the sea obeyed him.

In Matthew 14, when the wind was blowing Jesus kept quiet. When He commanded the wind and said peace be still, the wind and the sea obeyed Him, there was a great calm.

May God rise on your behalf today in the name of Jesus Christ. Every wind and sea tormenting your future, they will obey Him in the name of Jesus Christ.

Every poverty, sickness, witches and wizard, the issue of your status disturbing your family will obey Him in the name of Jesus Christ. Even the wind and seas obeyed Him, because He is the word, and He has the final say.

Eli fell because God kept silent over his life and started to speak to Samuel.

Thank Jesus He has spoken over your life and what He says is the final say, this year is your year of maximum.

While He has kept quiet over other people's matter He has spoken over yours.

This year is your year of maximum. The wind, sea, condition, circumstance, situation, government, and economy must obey Him. Where you have been minimum before, they must give you maximum because He has spoken.

Father, I thank you Lord for waking me up again, for not being quiet concerning my case.

Father, for what you have said concerning my future, concerning this year and this month, concerning my family and your church I am here to say thank you.

Thank him for what you are going to become. Not just things that will appear but for what we are going to become because of what He has said.

Father, for the things that I will become, that will appear I am here to say thank you.

Father, don't be quiet on my case, arise on my behalf, my family and the church and have mercy in the name of Jesus.

I decree: The Ancient of Days will arise on your behalf in the name of Jesus Christ. He will arise in mercy for you in the name of Jesus Christ.
And he saith unto them, Why are ye fearful, O ye of little faith? Then he arose, and rebuked the winds

and the sea; and there was a great calm (Matthew 8:26).

May God arise for you in the name of Jesus Christ. He rebuked the winds. Every winds rising against your destiny God will arise for you, there will be calmness in the name of Jesus Christ.

The men were amazed, and said, "What kind of a man is this, that even the winds and the sea obey Him (Matthew 8:27).

And there was in their synagogue a man with an unclean spirit; and he cried out, Saying, Let us alone; what have we to do with thee, thou Jesus of Nazareth? art thou come to destroy us? I know thee who thou art, the Holy One of God. And Jesus rebuked him, saying, Hold thy peace, and come out of him. And when the unclean spirit had torn him, and cried with a loud voice, he came out of him. And they were all amazed, insomuch that they questioned among themselves, saying, What thing is this? what new doctrine is this? for with authority commandeth he even the unclean spirits, and they do obey him (Mark 1:23-27).

Father, let all the powers in Heaven, on Earth and under the Earth obey your word regarding my maximum in name of Jesus.

All things in Heaven, on Earth and under the Earth must obey Him over your maximum. Everything must cooperate with you to ensure you get to your maximum because everything obeys Him. They are not the words of man they are the words of the Ancient of Days.

The number seven is the number for answer. The Bible says in 1 Kings 18:42-46, when there was no rain in the land for three and half years, God answered Elijah on the seventh occasion. God will not let you come down until your rain falls in the name of Jesus Christ.

Father, in my seventh month, in the month of July everything I have requested will appear in the name of Jesus.

Pray in the Holy Ghost for a minute.

My Prayer for You This Month:

Precious master, we thank you because everything obeys you. Take all the praise in the name of Jesus Christ. For arising on our behalf in mercy, take all the praise in the name of Jesus Christ. We decree upon the authority of your word concerning our 2015, let everything obey for our maximum in the name of Jesus Christ. Let all things in Heaven, on Earth and under the Earth obey in the name of Jesus Christ. We vow all the glory and praise to you. We dedicate July 2015 and the remaining days in 2015 to you in the name of the Father, Son and Holy Spirit in the name of Jesus Christ.

Prayer Charge For July:

From scripture and the operations of God we find a few things interesting on the seventh day.

Earlier, we noted that things might continue the way they are until God speaks; the moment He gets involved things must have a different outcome. Initially, darkness moved freely on the earth until God said, "Let there be light". Darkness was perambulating everywhere, roaming around, walking majestically, and parading the whole place, with no restriction. Darkness dominated everywhere. It continued until God spoke. Because He has the final say, everywhere obeys Him. I love what the scripture says in Mark 1:27, *And they were all amazed, insomuch that they questioned among themselves, saying, What thing is this? what new doctrine is this? for with authority commandeth he even the unclean spirits, and they do obey him.*

When people see what God is doing through you, people will question themselves, in the name of Jesus Christ. What was not done for others, because

God has gotten involved, they will do it for you in Jesus mighty name.

Every unclean spirit upon your way in 2015, you want to tell God to talk to them for you. Listen, there are issues you address yourself, there are issues God helps you to address. I'll give you an example, Jesus said, you shall say to this mountain, that means you are to do it yourself; but to Zerubbabel, God said "who are thou mountain" so instead of Zerubbabel talking, God talked for Zerubbabel. If they didn't obey you, they will obey God. You want to tell God, every unclean spirit upon my way, talk to them for me, and address them on my behalf.

Father, in this year 2015 especially in the month of July, every unclean spirit, and every satanic spirit upon my way, speak to them for me in the name of Jesus.

And the same day, when the even was come, he saith unto them, Let us pass over unto the other side (Mark 4:35).

He said we are passing over, we are not going under; you will never go under in Jesus name. If they're passing over, it means where they're going is a higher elevation. It doesn't matter, what appears on your way, you will go over them. If Satan comes your way, you will go over him, if a mountain comes your way you will go over it, because you're going higher. May God bestow upon you the ability to go over everything, so you can enter your maximum in Jesus mighty name.

Father, I receive divine ability to go over into my maximum in the name of Jesus.

In Mark 4: 36-40, the Bible says, *And when they had sent away the multitude, they took him even as he was in the ship. And there were also with him other little ships. And there arose a great storm of wind, and the waves beat into the ship, so that it was now full. And he was in the hinder part of the ship, asleep on a pillow: and they awake him, and say unto him, Master, carest thou not that we perish? And he arose, and rebuked the wind, and said unto the sea, Peace, be still. And the wind ceased, and there was a great calm. And he said unto them, Why are ye so fearful? how is it that ye have no faith?*

Pray that every fear that dominated your life last year, won't come near you this year; your life will be fear-free.

Father, every fear that I've experienced in the past vamoose; disappear, in the name of Jesus. Every fear troubling my future, troubling my tomorrow, my life, leave in the name of Jesus.

Many of us would have taken good steps in life, but fear did not let us. If the four lepers had submitted to fear, they would not have prospered in life. Through them, others discovered prosperity. Many of us would have done well in business, but for fear. Satan kept telling you, you were going to fail prevented you from going forward.

And they feared exceedingly, and said one to another, What manner of man is this, that even the wind and the sea obey him (Mark 4:41).

Father, in this year of Maximum, especially in the month of July, I speak to the Heavens, I speak to the earth and under the earth to cooperate with me for my maximum, support me for my maximum, in the name of Jesus. Heaven assist me, assist my family, and let all things cooperate with us, so we can get to our maximum.

I decree that everything in heaven and on earth, and under the earth will support, cooperate with you and help you to reach your maximum in the name of Jesus Christ.

Thank Him for what He has done and bless His name. Thank you Jesus, glory be to Jesus.

Your July 2015 is settled in the name of Jesus Christ.

Chapter Eight
August 2015

Hallelujah! We welcome everyone again into the presence of the Almighty God, on this Holy Mountain where He makes way for His people.

In Matthew 8:1-4, you will find the story of the man, who waited for Jesus to come down from the mountain. The Bible says the man was a leper and as soon as Jesus came down from the mountain, he approached Him for mercy, for an intervention, and to do for him what no man can do. As far as that man was concerned, everyone was running away from him because of his condition, so when the master returned from the mountain the man went to Him and fell down on his face to worship Him.

When Jesus returned from the mountain and met that man, Jesus gave to him what no man could have given to him. You can't come to the mountain, and not return with tangible things. May God of Heaven cause tangible things to be made manifest in your life henceforth in the name of Jesus Christ.

Everyone who has climbed this mountain has become a blessing to mankind on his or her return. You are on this mountain also and on your return, may the Ancient of Days make you a blessing to your generation in the name of Jesus Christ.

When you're on the mountain, you become a carrier of solution to those below the mountain. In Exodus 34:29, Moses returned with a package from God for His people. He returned with guidelines for the Israelites. He came back with something to affect generations eternally.

It's one thing to be blessed, it's another thing to be a blessing. To be blessed is not maximum, you're operating in average, not to be blessed is minimum, and to be a blessing is maximum.

If you are not blessed, your life will need to depend on the natural in order to make it. You will need to rely on "man's" effort. In Luke 5, there was a difference between the time Peter tried on his own, and the time Jesus said *Launch out into the deep, and let down your nets for a draught.* The blessing made the difference between both periods.

Blessing excuses you from labor, the day blessing comes your way, you will be excused from labor. Isaac had labored in Genesis 26, until God blessed him. As soon as the Ancient of Days blessed him, labor ceased and blessing showed up in form of prosperity and riches because *The blessing of the LORD, it maketh rich, and he addeth no sorrow with it* (Proverbs 10:22).

In the name of Yeshua the Son of God, because you have come to this mountain, may the blessing of the Ancient of Days manifest in you in the name of Jesus Christ.

To be blessed is to operate in average. He said to Abraham your father, in blessing I will bless you and I will make you a blessing, in you shall all the families of the earth be blessed. That is a man operating in maximum. I will not just bless you, in blessing I will bless you, in multiplying I will multiply you and in you shall all the families of the earth be blessed.

Until you become a blessing, you have not entered your maximum dimension.

May God use this mountain, to launch you out into becoming a blessing in the name of Jesus Christ, Amen!

The Bible says, it's more blessed to give than to receive. You are more blessed and you operate in the highest degree of blessing when you are a blessing. When Jesus returned from the mountain, according to Matthew 8, the leper ran to Him asking Him to do for him what no man can do.

What others are not capable of doing, may God put grace upon you to do such things in the name of Jesus Christ.

When you look at the story of Daniel, in Daniel chapters 1 & 2, you find the story of King

Nebuchadnezzar who had a dream. No matter how close you are to the person you are sleeping with on the same bed, you cannot tell their dreams.

Nobody can know the dream of another man, unless he operates in the level of the Gods.

Nebuchadnezzar had dreamt and in the bid to look for interpretation, discovered that his magicians, astrologers, Chaldean were liars. So he said to them, in order for me to believe your interpretation you must tell me the dream I dreamt. Only God can do that. No man can do such things; no man can operate at that level. In Daniel 2: 1- 11, when grace came upon Daniel, God gave Daniel the power to do what no man could do.

I prophesy: What men cannot do, God will put the grace in you to operate in such dimension in the name of Jesus Christ.

The God of Daniel, who is also your God, is the same yesterday, today and forever, He does not change.

I see God planting in you wisdom, understanding, and solutions for men in the name of Jesus Christ.

And the decree went forth that the wise men should be slain; and they sought Daniel and his fellows to be slain. Then Daniel answered with counsel and wisdom to Arioch the captain of the king's guard, which was gone forth to slay the wise men of Babylon: He answered and said to Arioch the king's captain, Why is the decree so hasty from the king? Then Arioch made the thing known to Daniel. Then Daniel went in, and desired of the king that he would give him time, and that he would shew the king the interpretation. Then Daniel went to his house, and made the thing known to Hananiah, Mishael, and Azariah, his companions: That they would desire mercies of the God of heaven concerning this secret; that Daniel and his fellows should not perish with the rest of the wise men of Babylon (Daniel 2:13-18).

May God show you mercy to know secret that others do not know in the name of Jesus Christ. The secret to escape being destroyed this year, especially this month of August may God deliver unto your life in the name of Jesus Christ.

Then was the secret revealed unto Daniel in a night vision. Then Daniel blessed the God of heaven (Genesis 1:19)

In the name of Jesus, may you also have cause to give thanks to God for the secret He will reveal to you in the name of Jesus Christ.

Then the king Nebuchadnezzar fell upon his face, and worshipped Daniel, and commanded that they should offer an oblation and sweet odours unto him. The king answered unto Daniel, and said, Of a truth it is, that your God is a God of gods, and a Lord of kings, and a revealer of secrets, seeing thou couldest reveal this secret. Then the king made Daniel a great man, and gave him many great gifts, and made him ruler over the whole province of Babylon, and chief of the governors over all the wise men of Babylon. Then Daniel requested of the king, and he set Shadrach, Meshach, and Abednego, over the affairs of the province of Babylon: but Daniel sat in the gate of the king (Daniel 2:46-49)

We see here, the power of being a blessing. Daniel was not only made great, he made way for his friends to be great. He became a blessing, and he began to operate in the highest level of blessing in Babylon.

In the name of Jesus may the grace to become a blessing be delivered to you in the name of Jesus Christ.

The number eight (8), which represents August stands for the power of maximum in being a blessing. Jesse had eight sons; the eighth star of Jesse is the man David. David was a man who operated in the highest level of maximum among men. So much so that when the Savior needed a family, He chose from the family of Jesse, through the generation of David. Which is why the King of kings is called "Jesus thou son of David".

David operated in such dimension because he became a blessing to his generation. *For David, after he had served his own generation by the will of God, fell on sleep, and was laid unto his fathers, and saw corruption: But he, whom God raised again, saw no corruption* (Acts 13:36)

In the name of Jesus, may God put in you what will make you be a blessing to your generation in the name of Jesus Christ.

In Mark 9:14-29; the other disciples who didn't go up the mountain could not be a blessing. They were blessed because they were Jesus' disciples, but they could not be a blessing to others. When Jesus came down from the mountain, Bible says as soon as the devil saw Jesus *it immediately threw the boy into a convulsion, he fell to the ground and rolled around, foaming at the mouth* (Mark 9:20,NIV). In verse 25, Jesus became a blessing, the disciples asked why they couldn't drive the Spirit out, and Jesus replied, *this kind can come forth by nothing, but by prayer and fasting* (Mark 9:29).

When you are on the mountain of fasting and prayer, God makes you a blessing. May God make you a blessing to your generation this year in the name of Jesus Christ.

The Bible says God gave Daniel wisdom to do what no man cannot do. They began to worship him like a God. The King, who was threatening to kill other people, fell down before him and began to worship him. When God puts in you what makes you a blessing, the world will fall down before you.

I see men falling down and bowing down before you just because of your God in the name of Jesus Christ.

When you are a blessing it becomes easy for men to agree that your God is God.

God's portion, plan and agenda for you this year is to make you a blessing.

Lift your voice and bless that God who has such plans for you, lift your voice and celebrate Him.

In Psalm 142:5, David said *I cried unto thee, O LORD: I said, Thou art my refuge and my portion in the land of the living.*

Father, I thank you for the portion you have reserved for me in this land of the living this year, especially this month of August, I thank you for my portion, the portion of my family, and your church in the name of Jesus Christ.

What will determine the height of your maximum is not what you have but who you become. Others may have what you have but they may never become what you become. In Genesis 26:12-14, Isaac had possessions but later the Bible said he became very great.

Father, in this year 2015, especially in the month of August, for what I will become, what my family and your church will become in our year of Maximum, I come to thank you.

In Daniel 2:17-19, Daniel asked for mercy from God. Everything you gain from God comes from the vehicle of mercy.

May this unchanging God reveal to you what will take you to the very top of your career in the name of Jesus Christ.

Father, I desire your mercy, show your mercy to me, show your mercy to my family, show your mercy to your church in the name of Jesus.

Daniel 6 shows us that Daniel got to the very top of affairs in the land of Babylon. So in his areas of life, God made him to enter into his maximum through great mercy.

Father, the mercy that will provoke, that will activate my maximum in all areas of life, pour that mercy upon me today in the name of Jesus Christ.

Then was the secret revealed unto Daniel in a night vision. Then Daniel blessed the God of heaven (Daniel 2:19).

Father, reveal to me the secret to maximum, in this year 2015, especially in the month of August in the name of Jesus.

Even though David had killed a bear and a lion in the past, he didn't enter into his maximum dimension in Israel until he slayed Goliath.

Father, the power to slay my Goliath so I can enter my maximum release unto me O Lord in the name of Jesus.

When he killed the lion and the bear, he was a blessing to himself, because those things would have killed him. When he killed Goliath, he was a blessing to his nation and the women began to sing, Saul has a slayed a thousand, but David 10,000.

O Lord my Father, I receive the power to slay every Goliath that will show up this year in the name of Jesus.

May God put in you His Spirit that will make you a Goliath killer in the name of Jesus Christ.

The number 8, which David stands for, is the number of Reserved Promotion. If it is a regular promotion anybody can get it, but if it is a reserved promotion, it's just for you.

We will ask God to reserve promotion for us this year. When Samuel went to the house of Jesse, according to 1 Samuel 16, he could have anointed anybody to be the king over Israel. He was going to anoint the first son, but God intervened. And if God had not intervened, he would have anointed any of David's brothers. Then he asked Jesse "don't you have another son?" Heaven resisted the anointing of any of David's brothers because that position was reserved for David.

Father, in this year 2015 especially in the month of August, make it my year and month of reserved promotion in the name of Jesus Christ.

May the Ancient of Days give you reserved promotion in the name of Jesus Christ.

Pray in the Holy Ghost.

My Prayer for You This Month:

Our Father in heaven we bless your name again and again for keeping us to see this month of August 2015.

Thank you for your plans and agenda to take us to maximum. Thank you for forbidding evil for us. Thank you for making our portion in the year a good portion in the land of the living. Glory and honor be to your wonderful name in the name of Jesus Christ.

Thank you for the prayers of your people. Thank you for mercy released to us to discover secrets in order to be a blessing to our generation. Lord, be glorified in the name of Jesus Christ.

O Father as you granted to Daniel all he requested, let our entire request be granted. Before today is over, make us come back to celebrate answers to our requests in the name of Jesus Christ. Make our joy full; turn all the readers of this devotional to Goliath killers. Make us a blessing to our generation in the name of Jesus Christ.

Let no man take our portion of our reserved promotion in the name of Jesus Christ. Disallow anyone that attempts it O Lord. As you disallowed Samuel and the brothers of David, disallow for us in the name of Jesus Christ. We vow all the praise to you. Glory to you O God, in Jesus mighty name we pray, Amen!! Hallelujah.

Prayer Charge For August:

One prayer you need to pray constantly is, Lord, open my eyes to see what is coming ahead of me. Friends, you will be confident that your year is settled if God opens your eyes slightly just to see a glimpse of what He has done. *Oh that men would praise the Lord for his goodness, and for his wonderful works to the children of men! For he hath broken the gates of brass, and cut the bars of iron in sunder* (Psalm 107:15-16). He did not say He will break the gate of brass, He said He had broken it; not that He will cut it; it is already cut.

Those women said, who would roll away the stone for us. Before they got there angels had rolled the stone away and sat on it. The angels had already taken care of what they were worried about. The angels sat on it to prevent it from rolling back because it was time for Jesus to leave the grave and enter His maximum.

Your angels will disgrace whatever stone says you won't enter into your maximum in the name of Jesus Christ. It is important for you to understand what God has done for you. This will increase and strengthen your faith for what He is yet to do. When David was shown Goliath, the giant, he said there was no giant there. He believed that because the One who delivered him from the paws of the lion and from the hands of the bear is the same One who would deliver this goliath into his hands. You must remember the things He has done to believe him for greater things ahead.

In 1 Samuel 16:11, *And Samuel said unto Jesse, Are here all thy children? And he said, There remaineth yet the youngest, and, behold, he keepeth the sheep. And Samuel said unto Jesse, Send and fetch him: for we will not sit down till he come hither.*

The first shall become last, and the last shall become the first.

Though David was the youngest he was the first as he was the choice. It doesn't matter where you are, if God has chosen you nobody can disqualify you.

1 Samuel 16:12, *And he sent, and brought him in. Now he was ruddy, and withal of a beautiful countenance, and goodly to look to. And the LORD said, Arise, anoint him: for this is he.* Praise God. 1 Samuel 16:13, *Then Samuel took the horn of oil, and anointed him in the midst of his brethren: and the Spirit of the LORD came upon David from that day forward. So Samuel rose up, and went to Ramah.*

If David hadn't received the Spirit in chapter 16, he won't have been able to fight Goliath in chapter 17. Because of the Spirit that came upon him as the eighth day man in chapter 16, he defeated Goliath hands down in chapter 17. Before we address our Goliath you want to say to the Almighty God, this year, especially in the month of August, let your Spirit come upon me mightily.

Father, by your spirit turn me into a goliath killer in the name of Jesus.

In 1 Samuel 17: 48, *And it came to pass, when the Philistine arose, and came and drew nigh to meet David, that David hasted, and ran toward the army to meet the Philistine.*

Goliath didn't know he was standing for the last time. He had been standing and standing for many years but this was his last stand. Every enemy standing before you today, they are doing their last in the name of Jesus Christ.

1 Samuel 17:49, *And David put his hand in his bag and took a stone and slang it and smote the philistine in his forehead, that the stone stuck in his forehead and fell upon his face to the earth.* This will be your story in the year 2015. *So did David prevail over the philistines with a stone and a sling and smote the philistine but there was no sword in the hand of David.* It means you don't need to go out to get anything, what you have already in your hand is enough to kill Goliath. You are going to say, Father, use what is in my hands today to kill my goliath.

Father, whatever is in my hands let it be sufficient, let it be enough to kill my goliath.

Goliath was not just a present or current enemy of David alone; He was also an enemy of the nation. It means what you have in your hands alone is enough to bring down Goliath. No wonder he said in Psalm 144:1, *blessed be the Lord my God which teacheth my hands to war and my fingers to fight*.

Also in Genesis 49:19 the Bible says, *Gad, a troop shall overcome him: but he shall overcome at the last.* It means no matter overcome you in the past, in accordance with the blessing of the eighth day which also stands for your eighth month, it is now your turn to overcome them even as Gad did in Jesus precious name.

Noah was called the eighth person. While everyone and their generation perished the eighth person was spared and his household. Upon the truth guiding this eighth month of August, throughout this year may we all be securely safe in the name of Jesus Christ.

May the blessings of this eighth month bring to us what the scripture refers to as divine substitution with others in Jesus wonderful name. Others will be punished for you, others will be beaten for you, and others will take the evil for you such that it will not come near your dwelling. While the uprising of waters swallowed others, the same lifted Noah and his household. What brings others down will raise you up in the name of Jesus Christ.

The scriptures say, when men are cast down then shall I say there is a lifting up (Job 22:29). It means you are not permitted to have the same experience; your experience must be different.

Father, we therefore dedicate the eighth day to you, this month of August 2015 in the name of the Father, in the name of the Son and of the Holy spirit. Blessed be your name. In Jesus precious name we pray. Shout an amazing Hallelujah.

Chapter Nine
September 2015

Hallelujah! We welcome you by His grace into the mountain of God's possibility. Where the ability of God, the Ancient of days, and your King can be experienced. It's important to know that until you come to the place where you can experience His ability you may never know the value of your God.

The value you place on something or somebody is usually determined by what it can do for you or who they are in your life. The performance and use of something determines its value, and the price. The more problems something can solve the more expensive they become.

Some jobs pay better than others because of the problems that one job or career can solve over the other. The ability to solve problems in life determines the value of a man.

In this year 2015, may God make you a problem solver for mankind in the name of Jesus Christ. Amen!

In Ephesians 3:20 the Bible says, *"Now unto him that is able to do exceeding abundantly above all that we ask or think, according to the power that worketh in us"*

You don't know what God is able to do until you come to the arena of prayer. Unto Him that is able to do exceedingly abundantly above all that we can ask or think. You can never know what He is able to do until you pray.

"God is able to do whatever He says He will do"...the ability of God, the power of God, the working of God; you cannot experience it until you come to the mountain of prayer. And that is why Paul in his writing in Ephesians 3:20 says to us *"unto Him that is able".*

Our God is able, and is able to do anything. The arena of prayers exposes you to the ability and wonders of God. Until you pray, until you live a life of prayer, you may never know what your God can do. And if you don't know what He can do, you may never know the value of your God.

The value everyone places on God is influenced by his or her faith. The ability to believe Him, to see what He can do determines their faith. That ability and knowledge of what He can do determines the value of God.

This is the reason why two people in the same nation value God differently. While Israel was struggling about whether to serve God or not, Joshua said, *"as for me and my house we will serve the Lord"*. Why would Joshua say so? It is because he had seen what God had done.

Joshua saw how God gave them the same land that giants dwelt and brought water out of the rock for them. He saw raw miracles in the wilderness. He saw God dividing up the Red sea. He saw how God fed them with quails, how He fed them with manna, and he saw how God provided for them.

In this month of September 2015 may God deliver giants into your hands in the name of Jesus Christ.

Every Red Sea upon your way to maximum, may God part them for you in the name of Jesus Christ.

May God close up the Red sea over every Egypt of your destiny in the name of Jesus Christ.

In this year 2015, God will provide for you in the name of Jesus Christ.

When you know His ability you will know His value. Nebuchadnezzar put the three Hebrew boys in the fire. They did not bow down to the image of the king. Not because they did not have reasons to be fearful for their lives, but they knew what their fathers had told them regarding what their God could do.

In the name of Yeshua the Son of God you will have many stories to tell people about what your God can do in the name of Jesus Christ. Amen!

Nebuchadnezzar made a mistake to threaten their God alongside with them. He said I will see the God who will deliver you from my hands. The reason why he could say that is because he did not know God and consequently, His value. He proceeded with his threats.

David wrote Psalm 34 because he had seen what God could do. He saw God deliver him from the lion, the bear, the hand of Goliath, and from the hand of Saul. He saw how God brought him into the palace, and showed him mercy and he said I will praise Him forever.

Knowing what He can do determines His value to you and His value will determine your praise to Him. Hannah did not sing until God opened her womb and then she sang. "There is none holy as the Lord; there is none besides thee. Neither is there any Rock like our God". Hannah began to compose songs because she saw what God could do.

In this year 2015, you will sing your own songs, you will compose your own songs, and you will release your own CD in the name of Jesus Christ.

Hannah didn't know the ability of God until she went to pray. When she had Samuel, and brought him back to God, she called him Samuel saying because I asked him of the Lord. She saw God's ability and the value of God was obviously real for her.

May you discover a new level of the value of your God in the Name of Jesus Christ.

His value can only be determined when you see what He can do. For with God all things are possible. And if with Him all things are possible, all possibility of value that a man can give, God qualifies for. All praise that any man can give, God qualifies for because with Him all things are possible.

Lift your voice and thank Him for all the things He has done in your life.

You want to lift your voice and thank Him for what you have experienced. David said for you have delivered me from the paws of the lion and the paws of the bear, I know what you can do. For everything He has done for you, for every "bear" He has delivered you from you will say:

Father for everything you've delivered me from in the past I'm here to thank you.

You want to thank Him for what He will do in your life in the year 2015, especially in the month of September. What eyes have not seen and ears have not heard.

In Ephesians 3:20, the Bible says, *"unto Him that is able to do exceedingly above all"*... so the ability to do maximum is in your God, when something is above all, it means maximum. So that means the power of maximum is in your God. You want to thank Him and say:

Father, for the power of maximum that you are going to display in my life, my family and your church, I am here to say thank you.

Life becomes challenging and the likelihood of been stranded is very high when you take steps in life without God's mercy being with you. Everyone admired in the scripture are people who obtained God's mercy. The scripture tells us that even Jacob, the third man in the line of God's covenant testified of God's mercy in Genesis 32:10:

"I am not worthy of the least of all the mercies and of all the truth which You have shown Your servant; for I crossed over this Jordan with my staff, and now I have become two companies."

Oh Father, let me find mercy in 2015, I will not just find mercy, mercy will find me, my family and your church in Jesus name.

I decree: In this particular month of September and all through 2015 you will find mercy and the mercy of God will find you in the name of Jesus Christ.

Revelation 22:1-2, *"And he showed me a pure river of water of life, clear as crystal, proceeding from the throne of God and of the Lamb. In the middle of its street, and on either side of the river, was the tree of life, which bore twelve fruits, each tree yielding its fruit every month. The leaves of the tree were for the healing of the nations."*

This means every month must produce for you. Every month must deliver for you.

Oh Father, in this month of September 2015, my life, work, and family will be productive. I will be fruitful, and I will bear fruits in Jesus name.

Ezra 10:9, *"So all the men of Judah and Benjamin gathered at Jerusalem within three days. It was the ninth month, on the twentieth of the month; and all the people sat in the open square of the house of God, trembling because of this matter and because of heavy rain."*

I decree concerning you: In this 9th month of September 2015, may your fruitfulness catch the attention of the world in the name of Jesus Christ.

May God give you enviable fruitfulness in the name of Jesus Christ.

The ninth month is the month people seek God. When people love God more.

Father, in this ninth month you will give me more reasons to love you, to seek you, and to serve you in Jesus name.

The Bible says the evil of a day is sufficient thereof, you want to decree:

Every evil in the year 2015, especially in the month of September stay away from me, go away from my family, my household and from the church of God in Jesus name.

Pray in the Holy Ghost for some minutes.

My Prayer For You:
Though you are the Invisible God, yet you manifest yourself in your children in strength,

wisdom, prosperity and in all ways. Yes, your works are truly visible. Please Father accept our thanks and praise in Jesus name. For the invisible strength you have given to everyone using this devotional I return all the glory and praise to you in the name of Jesus Christ.

May they go from strength to strength in Zion; I therefore decree unusual strength for you in the name of Jesus. What you will never be able to do humanly, because of the strength of heaven, begin to do them well in the name of Jesus Christ. Again we dedicate the month of September and all the days in it to you in the name of the Father, in the name of the Son and of the Holy Spirit. Glory and honor to your name Oh Lord. In Jesus name we pray.

Bless God for answered prayers.

Prayer Charge For September:

Listen friends, God never lifts anyone based on your faithfulness alone. The reason why you are considered faithful is because He is first faithful. He said when we are not faithful He abides faithful. No wonder David said in Psalm 89:1, *I will sing of the mercy of the Lord forever, with my mouth will I make known thy faithfulness to all generations.* The scriptures say, we love Him because He first loved us. Therefore, under the same scriptural principle, we are also faithful because He's first faithful.

In 2 Thessalonians 3:3, the Bible says, *'But the Lord is faithful, who shall stablish you, and keep you from evil'*. You are kept from evil because God is faithful. Every time you escape evil is a manifestation of the faithfulness of God. He said but the Lord is faithful, who shall establish you on the top. May the Lord establish your feet in the name of Jesus Christ.

What is the point of establishing you and exposing you to evil? He establishes you and makes sure that evil does not come near you.

Father, for every evil I have escaped, my family escaped, your church escaped in 2014 and all the past months in 2015 because of your faithfulness, I am here to say thank you Lord.

In 1 Thessalonians 5:24, *Faithful is he that calleth you, who also will do it*. Whatever He has called you to become, He will make sure you become it. God is the one that makes sure that whatever He has called you to be you become it. You don't become it because of your own labor. Rather, because He's faithful He makes sure whatever He has called you to become that He will also ensure that it is done.

We see an example in what He called Paul to become. Joseph didn't know he would become the Prime Minister. His dream didn't show he will become Prime Minister in Egypt, it only showed him his brothers will bow to him. He never knew that was in the plan. There are some things God will do with you that you have never dreamt about. He suddenly found himself in the palace. In the name of Yeshua the Son of God, you will reach your own palace in the name of Jesus Christ.

In 1 Timothy 1:12, Paul the Apostle said *"And I thank Christ Jesus our Lord, who hath enabled me, for that he counted me faithful, putting me into the ministry"*.

The Lord asked me to announce to somebody, in this month of September, your dream will come true. I don't know who you are; He said tell them in this year 2015, their dreams will come true. Your dream will come true.

Father, in the month of September, according to your word, let my dreams come true in the name of Jesus.

That means every dream of your life that has been delayed, as it were for Joseph, that there was a delay in his dream. Every delay of the past will not have influence in your 2015 again in the name of Jesus Christ.

When your dream comes true, your enemies are in trouble. The enemies saw Joseph and were disgraced. They were wondering how his dream would come true. When his dream came true they had to bow to him.

I decree: In the name of the One whose name is higher than any other name, every dream regarding your career, businesses, life, your personal life in the name of the Ancient One, your dream will come true in the name of Jesus Christ.

In Matthew 17, we see the story where Jesus took the disciples to the mountain of transfiguration. The highest experience with Jesus outside of the Holy Ghost coming on the day of the Pentecost was this experience. No higher experience, this was the maximum experience. They saw Jesus as in the days of His glory, pre-dissension to the earth. The Bible says, when they saw Him they said to Him, Master it is good that we are here, let us make three tabernacles, one for you one for Moses and one for Elijah, we don't want to go back home again.

Although He had twelve disciples, only three had that experience. Children can come from the womb; it doesn't mean they will have the same destiny. While nine remained at the bottom of the mountain, three went up. Jesus took three to the highest level.

Father, in this year 2015, especially in the month of September, take me higher, higher in you, higher in your power, higher in prayer, higher in experience, higher in anointing in the name of Jesus Christ.

All your blessings still in heavenly places in this 2015 will drop for you on the earth in the name of Jesus Christ. A man can receive nothing except it is given to him from heaven. Everything you need is in heaven; you only need heaven to pull it down. Every good and perfect gift comes from above, from the Father of Light with whom there is no variableness or shadow of turning.

Revelation 22:1, *'And he shewed me a pure river of water of life, clear as crystal, proceeding out of the throne of God and of the Lamb'*.

The origin of a blessing is very important. Here, it is coming from the throne of God and the Lamb. Every thing made from heaven always lasts, that is why He is called the Everlasting Father because things that come from Him last. Praise God. So the miracles that come from the Everlasting Father are everlasting miracles. The favor from the hands of the Everlasting Father is everlasting favor. The prosperity from the hands of the Everlasting Father is everlasting prosperity. That is why the Bible says whatsoever the Lord does shall be forever.

It is important that we comprehend the scriptures. If God gives you something, even with the devil running around he can't touch it. It is like when you put some corn seed in a bottle and tighten it and put it in a bird tree. The bird is unable to touch it. Likewise, you are secure because he that dwelleth in the secret place of the Most High shall abide under the shadow of the Almighty.

Revelation 22:2, *In the midst of the street of it, and on either side of the river, was there the tree of life, which bare twelve manner of fruits, and yielded her fruit every month: and the leaves of the tree were for the healing of the nations.* Every month something must happen to you, your fruit must abide. Your fruit must manifest, that means no month is permitted to be empty for you. Your life must produce monthly. It means no month must go empty every month must yield something. You are going to announce to September, September you have been programmed to yield for me, you will yield for me, you will yield for my family, and you will yield for the church.

Go on and thank Him for answered to prayers. Bless Him in the Holy Ghost.

Chapter Ten
October 2015

Hallelujah. We welcome everyone again to the presence of God where the Word of God says there's fullness of joy. Maximum joy is found and discovered in His Presence.

Psalm 16:11. Thou wilt shew me the path of life: in thy presence is fullness of joy; at thy right hand there are pleasures for evermore (Psalm 16:11)

Just as you find gas at the gas station, cars are sold at car dealership and we find toys sold at toy stores. In the same way when you come, truly come into His presence, you find maximum joy. His presence deposits into you the fullness of the joy of God.

In this year 2015, may God show you the way to His right hand in the name of Jesus Christ. May God show you direction to His right hand in the name of Jesus Christ.

In thy presence thou has shown me the path of life. As we saw in Psalm 16:11, there is a secret to life and that secret is found in His Presence. Peter was a man who was an experienced fisherman. One would expect that he would know a good place to fish, where all the fishes were located. However, we find out that it doesn't matter what you know because what you know is always limited. What He knows is unlimited or maximum in expression.

I decree concerning you this year especially in the month of October, may you encounter joy at its fullest in the name of Jesus Christ. May you come in contact with joy at its maximum in the name of Jesus Christ.

You are exposed to two things when you are in His presence: **Fullness of joy** and **pleasure forevermore**. So, being in His presence brings you joy beyond the measure you could ever imagine. It brings you to a new depth and height of joy that you can never fathom. It brings you to a new level of quality and quantity of joy that you can never think about.

When Jesus gave the parable about the lost sheep He said if a man has 100 sheep and loses one, then searches for it diligently and finds it, when he finds it he runs with joy and calls his neighbors to come rejoice with him.

In this year 2015, neighbors, family and friends and the body of Christ will come and rejoice with you in the name of Jesus Christ.

When you become restored, through His involvement, His presence and ability brings you the fullness of joy. Hannah came sad but the Bible says the presence of God swallowed up her sorrow, sadness, and bitterness; the Bible says she was no longer sad. Joy took over.

Wherever bitterness, sorrow and sadness are sitting over your life, joy is taking over in the name of Jesus Christ.

In John 21, Jesus found the disciples trying to fish after their Master had been crucified. They lacked understanding of the scripture that He had risen. He found them where the distraction of life had caged them.

Wherever life has caged you, I prophesy to you today, you are coming out of those cages in the name of Jesus Christ.

John 21:4-5, *but when the morning was now come, Jesus stood on the shore: but the disciples knew not that it was Jesus. Then Jesus saith unto them, Children, have ye any meat? They answered him, No.*

Jesus will address every emptiness of your life and destiny in the name of Jesus Christ. That womb that appears empty, that home that appears devoid of children, that life that appears spouseless, that business that appears empty, every space in His church that appears vacant, the Lord will address it in the name of Jesus Christ.

Verse 6, And he said unto them, Cast the net on the right side of the ship, and ye shall find. They cast therefore, and now they were not able to draw it for the multitude of fishes.

I prophesy this year 2015 especially in October He will introduce you to the right side in the name Jesus Christ.

Where they had labored and life gave them a "no" Jesus introduced them to the right side.

Say Father show me the right side.

What is lost is always found at the right side. May God bring you to the right side in the name of Jesus Christ. At the right side, you leave minimum or emptiness, and go into maximum.

I prophesy to you again wherever you have lost direction to the right side of the Father, because of His presence, you are relocating to His right side again in the name of Jesus Christ.

And the whole multitude of the people were praying without at the time of incense. And there appeared unto him an angel of the Lord standing on the right side of the altar of incense. And when Zacharias saw him, he was troubled, and fear fell upon him. But the angel said unto him, Fear not, Zacharias: for thy prayer is heard; and thy wife Elisabeth shall bear thee a son, and thou shalt call his name John (Luke 1:10-13).

Anywhere you hear the Bible refer to "right hand", good is always happening there. The right hand of God will locate you in the name of Jesus Christ. Because of His right hand mercy will locate you in the name of Jesus Christ.

Say: My angel come to the right side of my life and destiny in the name of Jesus Christ.

The disciples were looking for fish and He showed them the right side. They were looking for signs He showed them the right side. It is very important for you to understand the blessings of the right hand or right side.

We have heard with our ears, O God, our fathers have told us, what work thou didst in their days, in the times of old. How thou didst drive out the heathen with thy hand, and plantedst them; how thou didst afflict the people, and cast them out. For they got not the land in possession by their own sword, neither did their own arm save them: but thy right hand, and thine arm, and the light of thy countenance, because thou hadst a favor unto them (Psalm 44:1-3)

Having possessions in life is not by the strength of your sword or the labor of your hand. Possessions in life is gotten by the right hand of God.

Two people were hung with Him on the cross one on the right and the other on the left. They both ended up in different places.

Anytime you are on His right hand you are always favored. Throughout 2015 especially in this month of October you will be on the right hand of God in the name of Jesus. I see God locating you from the other side of life to His right hand in the name of Jesus Christ. You will gather mightily because God's right hand is where fullness of joy and pleasure is found.

Psalm 80:17, *Let thy hand be upon the man of thy right hand, upon the son of man whom thou madest strong for thyself.*

When you see the hand of God upon the life of a man, you know that that man has found favor in the sight of the Lord. And once His hand is upon you, you will outrun the impossible. In 1 Kings 18:46 when God's hand was upon Elijah he outran chariots.

God always makes strong the people on His right hand. That's why Jesus himself is seated at the right hand of the Father. Psalm 110:1 *The Lord said unto my Lord, Sit thou at my right hand, until I make thine enemies thy footstool.*

I prophesy to someone today may you be given your seat at the right hand. Anytime you are given a seat at His right hand you are given a seat in victory.

Whatever has troubled and defeated you in the past, because you have found a seat at the right hand of God, you are defeating all your enemies hands down in the name of Jesus Christ.

One of the benefits of His presence is the privilege of locating His right hand. You don't only have fullness of joy; you also locate His right hand.

When you find His right hand you find His power. The power of God is located on His right hand. The Bible says in Psalm 118: 15-16 *But truly I am full of power by the spirit of the Lord, and of judgment, and of might, to declare unto Jacob his transgression, and to Israel his sin.*

Jesus saith unto him, Thou hast said: nevertheless I say unto you, Hereafter shall ye see the Son of man sitting on the right hand of power, and coming in the clouds of heaven (Matthew 26:64).

If anything must change for you, your position must move to His right hand this year. But you can't relocate until you are filled with or you find His presence. Our prayer this month will be focused on having His presence be with us.

The Bible said in John 3:1-2 *There was a man of the Pharisees, named Nicodemus, a ruler of the Jews: The same came to Jesus by night, and said unto him, Rabbi, we know that thou art a teacher come from God: for no man can do these miracles that thou doest, except God be with him.*

We see in Acts 10:38; *How God anointed Jesus of Nazareth with the Holy Ghost and with power: who went about doing good, and healing all that were oppressed of the devil; for God was with him*

Throughout this year 2015 especially this month of October, may God and His presence be with you in the name of Jesus Christ.

Lift your voice and begin to thank Him.

Thank Him for His plan of pleasure and not of pressure this year, especially this month.

Eyes have not seen, ears have not heard, neither has it entered the heart of any man. Whatever God will do, will always be above and beyond our imagination.

Thank Him for all the wonders waiting for you, your family and His church this year and especially this month of October.

David said goodness and mercy shall follow me.

Father, in this year 2015, my year of maximum, in this land of the living, may your goodness and mercy follow me and my family all the days of our lives.

May His goodness and mercy be your companion this year.

Father, all through the year 2015 especially in the month of October let your presence be with me and my family in the name of Jesus Christ.

The first blessing of His presence is fullness of joy. That is joy at maximum.

Father, in this year 2015, especially this month of October make my joy full, full to the maximum in the name Jesus Christ.

Scripture says God's hand is upon the man of His right side.

Father, move me, my family and your church to your right side in the name Jesus Christ.

Father, as you move me to your right side, I will locate abundance of prosperity, in the name of Jesus Christ.

Father, by your right hand favor me, my family, your church in the name of Jesus Christ.

Father, as you go before me this year, let your fire consume every evil upon my path in the name of Jesus Christ.

Pray in the Holy Ghost.

My Prayer for You This Month:

We give you praise and thanks for everything you have done regarding this year especially the month of October. Thank you for mercy, thank you for moving us to the right side. Thank you for your right hand that has shown us favor. Glory, honor be to your wonderful name O God. Let all the prayers be answered in the name of Jesus Christ. Let your mercy pursue and overtake us in the name of Jesus Christ. In this month of October make all things well in the name of Jesus Christ. We dedicate this month of October 2015 and the entire year unto you in the name of the Father, the Son and the Holy Spirit. Thank you Father Lord, in Jesus mighty name we pray, Amen!

Prayer Charge for October

The word assurance must be impressed in our Spirit. We must be well assured of our tomorrow. Let faith arise in your hearts for tomorrow, because what you cannot believe you cannot receive. He that cometh to God must believe that He is and is a rewarder of them that diligently seek Him. This means how much of belief I have will determine how much I will receive.

Lets take a look at some scriptures. In Hebrews 10: 21-22a, *and having an high priest over the house of God; Let us draw near with a true heart in full assurance of faith, having our hearts sprinkled from an evil conscience.* Don't come to God unless you are full of assurance.

That is why even though Job was pressed, he was assured. Somebody that life had beaten down was assured his Redeemer lives.

There is something to do to enter maximum. The story of Elijah affords us an excellent example.

Elijah's time was up and Elisha was well positioned. There's a position you ought to be in, to enter maximum. If you want to visit the gallery of a building, access to the gallery will be limited to certain areas. So, to get there, you would have to look for where the right access point, and if you are at the wrong access point, you won't reach your destination. You can be on the wrong side of maximum you need to be on the right side. Lift your voice and pray one more time:

Father, I call upon you now, place me on the right side for maximum in the name of Jesus.

As they went from Gilgal to Bethel, from Bethel to Jericho, from Jericho to Jordan, Elijah said to Elisha, *tell me what I can do for you before I am taken away.* Elisha responded *please let me inherit a double share of your spirit and become your successor* (2 Kings 2:9-10, NLT). The man minimized his request, he asked for double when he could have asked for triple. Do you know the reason he was given double was because that was what he believed for? You determine your maximum not God. He kept telling me, Elisha could have been ten times of Elijah but what he asked for was double because his faith could not carry it. You want to pray:

Father, pour upon me the available spirit of faith in Heaven that will take me and guarantee my highest maximum in the name of Jesus.

You have asked a difficult thing, Elijah replied. If you see me when I'm taken from you, then you will get your request. But if not, then you won't. (2 Kings 2:10)

When his request was going to be granted there was something he had to do. He said, if you see me, you will attain your maximum. There is always something to do. Jesus said to Mary and Martha, Martha you are worried about too many things, only one thing is needful and Mary has secured it. As Mary secured her own, may you secure your one needful thing in the name of Jesus Christ.

Let me give an example, for Hannah's womb to be open, she could have done any other thing but all she needed to do was make a pledge to God, If you give me this boy I will give him back to you. That is all she needed to do. She had done so many other things, cried, and was bitter. You have done too many things that are not required. It is like somebody who wants to graduate college and has completed all elective requirements without completing the mandatory requirements. You want to become a doctor but you studied Yoruba, French and Spanish and you submit your "intent to graduate" because you have sufficient credits, it is not the quantity of credits, it is the quality of credits.

What was required of Elisha? To see Elijah. What is required for you is not what is required of your neighbor, so you don't do what your neighbor is doing. You don't know their requirements. The fact that you are in the same college doesn't mean you are studying the same course. Given this, do not depend on what your neighbor is doing. That is why it is wrong to imitate people. If you live their life you run the risk of dying their death. You have to do your own thing. Ask God for what you need to do to enter into your maximum.

Father, whatever it may be that I need to do to enter my highest maximum, help me Father to do them in the name of Jesus.

Without an Elijah, Elisha could not discover his maximum, without a Moses, Joshua could not discover his maximum, without Jesus, Peter could not discover his maximum.

Father, whosoever I need to meet to enter my maximum, may we discover ourselves, may we encounter ourselves, may we meet together in the name of Jesus.

Father, we know with full assurance that October is truly secured, even November is truly secured, and December is truly secured. Lord, we know that signs do not need to take long before they begin to happen after prayer. Father, let the signs begin immediately. We dedicate October to you again in the name of the Father, Son and Holy Spirit. Thank you again Holy Father, in Jesus name we pray.

Chapter Eleven
November 2015

Hallelujah!!! We welcome everyone again into the presence of the Ancient of Days, where God answers prayers and proves that He is the Almighty. Where He proves that all powers in Heaven and on Earth belong to Him. Where God makes way for His people. A place where His name alone is glorified. A place where life's destiny is completed. A place where the joy of many is made full. A place where people enjoy divine intervention. A place where everyone agrees He is Lord.

We have to understand that God is the Almighty and whenever He wants to prove Himself, He uses the avenue of prayer to answer His people.

In the Bible, we see a nation that God loved but who began to despise Him by going after other gods like Baal. As it were, God always has a remnant that serves as agents of change for the generation.

This year, I see God making you an agent of change in the name of Jesus Christ.

For every high priest taken from among men is ordained for men in things pertaining to God, that he may offer both gifts and sacrifices for sins (Hebrews 5:1).

When God wants anything done, He looks for a man to use.

Also I heard the voice of the Lord, saying, Whom shall I send, and who will go for us? Then said I, Here am I; send me. (Isaiah 6:8)

May God find you useful this year in Jesus name.

When the nation of Israel turned against God, Elijah the Tishbite was a man that God found. He was set-aside for this purpose. So when Israel turned to Baal for help, God put the burden in Elijah to call Israel together. May God put the burden that will cause nations to submit to you inside of you in Jesus mighty name.

The God you serve, answers by fire. His superiority over other gods is His ability to answer prayers, while others can't answer prayers. He alone answers prayers.

I decree: In this year 2015, your God will show His superiority above every other God in the name of Jesus Christ.

He allowed the prophets of Baal to go ahead and pray to their gods. They have eyes but can't see, have ears but can't hear, have hands but can't do anything but the Lord God whom we serve can see, hear and saves.

Anyone contending with your God will be disappointed and disgraced this year.

I see groups of people on the earth today ganging up against our God. They should ask the prophets of Baal, only if they knew, they would not do what they are doing. Through His church, He will manifest His glory in the name of Jesus.

Elijah came onto the scene and called upon the name of the Lord our God. *And he put the wood in order, and cut the bullock in pieces, and laid him on the wood, and said, Fill four barrels with water, and pour it on the burnt sacrifice, and on the wood* (1 Kings 18:33)

He put the wood in order. In this year 2015, everything not in order in your life, the God of order will put them in order for you in the name of Jesus.

Why does your God answer your prayers, and the prayers of His people? He answers because He is a covenant keeping God. In this 2015, may the God of Abraham, Isaac and Israel answer your prayers in the name of Jesus.

In this year 2015, the Lord will do something in your life that will be visible for the world to see in the name of Jesus.

The world will agree with you and your Lord. In this year 2015, the enemies of Jesus will run into hiding. Anything contrary to the altar of the Lord our God, will go into extinction in the name of Jesus.

Through the power of prayers, all the enemies of Israel were slain. I see all your enemies slain in 2015 in the name of Jesus.

And it shall come to pass, that before they call, I will answer; and while they are yet speaking, I will hear (Psalm 65:24). He will decorate your 2015 with answers in the name of Jesus.

He proved He is the God of Elijah. The good news is that He doesn't change. He answered the prayer of Hannah, the widow of Nain, the prayers of Bartimaeus, the prayers of Paul and Silas. He will answer your prayers in the name of Jesus.

He doesn't just answer prayers but He answers prayers colorfully.

Now unto him that is able to do exceeding abundantly above all that we ask or think, according to the power that worketh in us. (Ephesians 3:20)

He doesn't just answer what you say but also answers what you think.

And it shall come to pass, that before they call, I will answer; and while they are yet speaking, I will hear (Psalm 65:24). Before you ask He has answered.

Delight thyself also in the LORD; and he shall give thee the desires of thine heart (Psalm 37:4).

He grants desires. May your desires this year be granted in the name of Jesus. In this 2015, men will come together to document your story and God will advertise Himself through your prayers in the name of Jesus.

All you need to do is ask. The only way you will not receive, is if you do not ask.

For every one that asketh receiveth; and he that seeketh findeth; and to him that knocketh it shall be opened (Matthew 7:8).

Hitherto have ye asked nothing in my name: ask, and ye shall receive, that your joy may be full (John 16:24).

Jesus said you have not asked enough. Ask in His name so that your joy may be full.

We have asked for January to October, it is time to ask again. Lift up your voice and thank the Lord who answers prayers.

We want to thank Him again for all the prayers He has answered in the past and all the prayers He is yet answer.

Father, for all the prayers you have answered and all the prayers you are yet to answer this year, I am here to say thank you.

Father, for testimonies already waiting for me, my family and your church this year, especially in the month of November, I am here to say thank you.

When He answers the prayers of the people, they always sing Him a new song.

1 Samuel 2:1 tells us of the new song Hannah sang to the Lord, *And Hannah prayed, and said, My heart rejoiceth in the LORD, mine horn is exalted in the LORD: my mouth is enlarged over mine enemies; because I rejoice in thy salvation.*

Father, thank you for new songs you have for me this year, especially this month of November 2015.

The platform of divine involvement is mercy. Where mercy is not found, God is not involved. He only gets involved in the case of people who cry out for mercy.

Father, in this year 2015, especially in this month of November, have mercy upon me, my family and your church in the name of Jesus Christ.

Father, make this year 2015 and especially the month of November, my year of answers. Give me all the answers I have been waiting for this year in the name of Jesus Christ.

In Luke 1:8-14 as the Lord made that year the year of answers for Zachariah, He will also make this year your year of answers in the name of Jesus.

Father, make this year 2015, the year of answers for me, my family and your church in name of Jesus.

When the fire fell for Elijah, the eyes of all saw it.

Father, this year do visible and undeniable things in my life, in my family and in your church in the name of Jesus Christ.

Father, disgrace and disappoint, every enemy of Jesus in my life, my family, our nation and your church in the name of Jesus Christ.

Father, in this year of 2015, especially in the month of November, do things in my life, my family and in your church that will make nations bow to you in the name of Jesus Christ.

Father, in this year 2015, especially in November, introduce me to a new level of prosperity that I have never imagined in the name of Jesus Christ.

Father, introduce me to a new level of influence that many will come to know and serve you in the name of Jesus Christ.

Pray in the Holy Ghost.

My Prayer For You This Month

Father, we adore you again and again. To you alone are all praises due. To you alone are all honor due. We honor and glorify you for all you have done. Thank you for this year and especially for this month, November. Take all the glory and praise in the name of Jesus Christ. May the effect of your undeniable mercy be upon our life, destiny, family, and your church in the name of Jesus Christ. Make this year, our year of many answers in the name of Jesus Christ. Make this our year of maximum answers in the name of Jesus Christ. Give us a foretaste of what you are about to do in our lives even in many, many years to come. Glory, honor be to your wonderful name O God. We dedicate the month of November onto you in the name of the Father, the Son and the Holy Spirit. Blessed be your name, in Jesus precious name we pray.

Prayer Charge For November

Our thanksgiving must be greater in quantity, quality and effort than our prayer request.

Ephesians 3:20 says, *Now unto him that is able to do exceeding abundantly above all that we ask or think, according to the power that worketh in us.* If He is going to answer all the prayers you have asked, He deserves all the thanksgiving you can ever offer; you must offer maximum thanksgiving. In the name of Yeshua the Son of God, everything you have asked Him, may God give to you in the name of Jesus Christ.

He does not only give what you have asked for; He also gives us what we think about. You have been thinking of beginning a project, and have no family budget allocated for it, but you have been thinking about where the funds for the project will come from. Suddenly, someone brings you the funds you need for the project. You'll wonder how that could be, since you have not prayed about the need for the money yet, you've just been thinking about it.

This means we owe Him thanksgiving not only for what we ask, but also for what we think. His word says He is going to do *exceeding abundantly above* it. So, after you thank Him for what you have asked, and thought, you should thank Him for blessings above those, because we know that He is able to do exceeding abundantly above what you have asked and thought about.

In a nutshell, the three dimensions of thanksgiving are, thanksgiving for what you have asked, thanksgiving for what you are thinking of and thanksgiving for above what you have thought. Which is why your thanksgiving must always be more than your prayer points.

The day your prayer points exceed your thanksgiving you have not prayed well; if you pray well your thanksgiving will always exceed what you have requested. You should always thank Him for everything you have asked, for the things you think He is going to do and for His ability to do exceeding abundantly above all.

It is good to understand how prayer works, you cannot commit to thanksgiving and ever be stranded in life. The eleventh son of Jacob, who was Joseph, was the first son to prosper exceedingly. Until they came to Egypt, Jacob was still laboring and laboring. When they were coming to Egypt, he brought all his children's children because they couldn't feed on their own, seventy of them.

Jacob was housing seventy people that were relocating; they were not going to be working, and they were going to be dependent on Joseph. This shows how much God had blessed Joseph.

You want to pray a very serious prayer: **Lord, bless me until I become a blessing, don't stop blessing me until I become a blessing**.

If God blesses you, and you are not a blessing to others, people will hate you with your blessing. They will say who is he? He is just bragging. What does he have? How do we know he is not stealing? If you gave them money they will never say you are stealing. If you pay their children's school fees, you are a good man. We have never seen a kind of man like that. They will say God will keep you for us, you are a blessing; you are an angel sent to our family. Don't forget what they said about Joseph, they were going to kill him, and they were going to make sure his dream wouldn't come true. When he gave them money and food, he was the best man among their family, you would think he was the first-born though he was the eleventh born. You will tell God, don't stop blessing me until I become a blessing.

Father, please don't stop blessing me until I become a blessing, not just in my family but also

to strangers and to nations in the name of Jesus Christ.

Until Joseph, some of the prophecies that God spoke unto Abraham never happened. God had promised that nations who don't know your God would serve you. It didn't happen to Abraham, rather, they chased Abraham. It didn't happen to Isaac. It didn't happen to Jacob himself, the first son it happened to was Joseph.

Father, every promise that has never happened in my family, every blessing that has never manifested in my family let it manifest in me.

Every one in Egypt served him including Pharaoh, who said I am going to put you in the second throne and through your hands all of Egypt will eat. With this statement, Pharaoh unknowingly placed himself in the hands of Joseph since he was part of "all of Egypt." And so Joseph, the son of Jacob became a blessing and a solution to the entire nation.

Father, every blessing that has never manifested in my family, in this year 2015

manifest it in me and manifest it in my destiny in the name of Jesus Christ.

Joseph was not just a solution to a people; he was a solution to the entire world. It is good to be a solution; people will look for you. Before our friend, Dr. Myles Munroe died last year, he was a blessing to the entire world. Just last year he had 760 invitations to speak. If he accepted every invitation, he would need two to three years to finish his engagements for that year. God made him a world-level solution that the world always sought after him.

Father, put something in me that the world will look for.

Your value in life is not how you look, it is what you give and what you can offer. When you are employed, it is because of what you can offer them. Joseph was such a blessing; Pharaoh said to him, I give the whole nation to you that was his value. If they were going to pay him a salary, his salary was equivalent to Egypt; he gave him the whole Egypt because of what God put in him. Even Pharaoh said, where can such a man in whom the Spirit of God is be found? God put something in him.

Father, put something in me that will solve the world's problem, so the world will look for me for solution in the name of Jesus.

Look at the story of the Syrian man called Naaman; Syria and Israel had no relationship from ages past. When the General Naaman needed a solution, the maid girl told him there was a prophet in our village, if you go to him no matter what disease you have, he has a solution. The man didn't want to go but looked at his leprosy and thought let him give the prophet a try.

People have gone to places that didn't work for them because they were looking for solutions. If you hear what people have done for solutions you will be amazed. One of my pastor friends gave me a testimony: he said his father was very rich when he was growing up. His father bought him a car and his fetish girlfriend suggested they go see someone. She took him to a particular man, who said because of the riches of his father, people were against him since he was the apparent heir to the blessings of his father. He said they had to fortify him and the car. So they gave him something to put in the car. The night he put the 'thing' in the car, was the night the car got stolen. When the car didn't have any 'fortification' it was not stolen. He said that's when he knew that all these people were liars. What people do to fortify themselves, you will surprised and shocked but when God makes you a solution even when they don't like your face they will still come to meet you.

Father, put in me what will solve the world's problem.

Don't just desire to solve the problem of the people around you. Sometimes you should think beyond your career. Dr. Myles Munroe didn't go to college to learn how to talk but God put something in him. Your career is good but when God blesses you, your career can't explain the blessings God has given you.

If you can explain what you have, it didn't come from God. If you can explain how you bought your car now, it didn't come from God. You can say glory be to God but your money paid for it. We are not talking about little blessings, buying cars, houses; you don't need even to pray to have those, just have good credit you can buy all those things. We are talking about something that money cannot buy. I'm not saying don't give glory to God for your cars but you don't need prayer to buy all those things. If you live eternally you can never qualify for it, those are the things I want you to pray for.

Father, put something in me that will solve the world's problem in the name of Jesus.

I believe there are two ways God blesses people; He blesses His children by covenant, and He blesses unbelievers by chance. The young girl from Pakistan, Malala Yousafzai, the Nobel peace prize winner, now meets with national leaders, presidents and kings everywhere. God gave her opportunity. Even I saw the picture she took with the U.S. president, he shook her with both hands. She had a solution to the world. Bill Clinton was the poorest governor when he was the governor of Arkansas; he became president he didn't make it. According to the Clinton's, they left the white house in debt but today he controls about several millions of dollars through his foundation because he had a vision to solve world's problem in the area of health, AIDS. And people are committing their fortunes into his hands. Don't think it is this job that you are doing, that you will do until you die; there will be a time if you don't leave the job, the job will leave you. Do you want to die after you retire? There is something you must be doing in life, you must be a solution. That is how to live the rest of your life. That is how to plan for the future. Thank God for the money you are being paid now, but there will be a time if you don't go they will ask you to go. Then what will you be do with the rest of your life?

That is why you want God to make you a solution. This way, your life will keep increasing as you age in the name of Jesus. When I saw Bill Clinton, I said his life is more valuable today than ever. Not just to America but to the entire world especially Africa. He goes to speak somewhere they pay him a several thousands of dollars. And they beg him, to accept a speaking engagement. He was going to speak in a country, they paid him several thousands of dollars to speak for an hour and he's just talking. The things he said you can say it but you don't have that opportunity. You are going to pray to God, and ask Him to make you a solution, whatever it may take.

Father, whatever it will take make me a solution to the world, give me a problem to solve for the world, just one problem to solve for the world.

Pray in the Holy Ghost.

Warren Buffet and Bill Gates, run their foundations. Now they are funding the Clinton foundation because of the good job he is doing. The quality of your life is not what you have but the problem you have solved. Anybody can become an influence in the world. Even the Pope wanted to meet with Malala. Some people are saying she's the next mother Theresa. I sat down and said to God, Lord tell me something that will make 2015 a difference. He said it is in you solving people's problems. When you solve people's problem you will always be lifted. Make up your mind that this year will be different. You must be a solution to people; people must look for you when they need something. Even for the things you can't solve, you should be a resource to recommending a solution. That is how God should make you. Prayer for good food is good but you don't need prayer for those things. God is committed to your daily bread, He said give us this day our daily bread. You become bread to others, when they are looking for satisfaction, when they see you; they say just seeing you has solved their problems.

Lord, what better way to speak to us because we have no other example of solution but you. You do not solve earthly problems alone, you solve eternal problems. No matter what names we throw out there, they may have solved a lot of earthly problems but nobody can solve eternal problems but you. So you are the highest of the maximum and that is why we want you. There's no doubt you said the entire year 2015 is settled.

You said but let the people understand what can make it a different year for them. That as this year draws to an end, they are not only thanking me for their lives, but others are thanking me on their behalf that they are alive because they are and remain a blessing to them.

Before Joseph died, he told the children of Israel that when he dies and God fulfills His promise to take them out of Egypt, they should take his bones from Egypt, and carry it with them. If he didn't do well they would have put his bones in the trash. Because he was their solution, while they were going, he was the only dead person that left Egypt.

They were carrying his bones until they got to the Promised Land. He was the only dead man in the Promised Land. When you are a solution, you are remembered even when you are gone. Lord make us a blessing in Jesus precious name. Thank you Jesus.

This is the depth of our request, that you give us the ability to be a solution to one of the world's problems. We will do well in this end time with evangelism if we solve human problems because the world will ask about our story so we can tell them you are the One that made our story look like this.

All the folks whose names we have mentioned are people that chance and opportunity happened to.

Imagine if God raised you up to solve problems related to AIDS. The world would want to know their story. We can then tell them "it is Jesus who has changed my life". The recipients of that solution would want to serve their God. Oh God of Heaven, this is our burden. **Father, raise solutions out of here in the name of Jesus Christ. Make us a factory of solution in the name of Jesus Christ.**

Blessed be your name.

For God to equip you to solve a nation's problem, you must be solving a neighbor's problem first. Some of us don't know God checks how faithful we have been with what He gives us. He that is faithful with little, much more shall be committed to his hands. Make up your mind to help the people you see around you to solve their problems. When God sees how well you are doing, He will then keep on expanding your coast.

Jesus wants to be highly glorified in these end times. He is looking for those to use, who will say, God I am available. It reminds of the song Alpha and Omega, it was commonly sung in one of the African countries. However, when Israel Houghton sang it the song leapt to its next level. Even what men have invented before, by the reason of your use and modification of that thing, the world will hear about your God in the name of Jesus Christ.

Lord, let the spirit of problem solving; let the grace of problem solving which was upon Jesus let it be upon us. Jesus said *behold the Lamb of God that has come to take away the sins of the world.* Lord, you solved the problem of sin, what nobody could solve, you came as a lamb and solved it. Now the entire world is looking at you for salvation.

Oh my God, put in us the spirit and the grace that will solve problem for mankind in the name of Jesus Christ. No matter what technology has seen now, there are things yet to be invented and it is people that will invent it. Inventors are not just scientists they are thinkers. Lord put in our mind inventions in the name of Jesus Christ. In our sleep let us see inventions in the name of Jesus Christ. When we are talking to people in normal conversations, what they are saying, magnify it in our ears and heart in the name of Jesus. Make us a company of solutions in the name of Jesus Christ.

We are prepared for what you want to do in the rest of this year. One thing we want to ask, if there is any area of our life that we are not yet prepared, please prepare us in the name of Jesus Christ. Thank you Holy Father in Jesus mighty name we pray.

Chapter Twelve
December 2015

Welcome to the presence of God where all things are possible. All things are not possible everywhere. The only place where things are possible is in His presence. It's important to know there are locations in life that limit you naturally from achieving certain things, but when you are in His presence it is a place without limitation. Matthew 19:26b tells us that *but with God all things are possible.*

If God is involved you can be sure all things are possible. It means your maximum in 2015 is possible because God is here. With man it may be impossible but with God it isn't. The involvement of God in the matter will determine the type of outcome you will receive.

This year especially this month of December, may God take you to heights He won't take others. In Mark 9, out of twelve disciples Jesus only took three disciples to the Mount of Transfiguration. During this time, a man brought his son to the disciples for healing; the disciples had no answer to his problem. As soon as Jesus arrived, Satan ran away quickly once he saw Jesus.

Every Satanic power and that of the kingdom of darkness that has troubled you in the past is running away quickly in the name of Jesus Christ.

The nine disciples combined couldn't solve the problem but as soon as Master Jesus was involved the devil ran away. When He is involved all things are possible.

No matter what promise you have been given regarding your 2015, you should know ALL things are possible. It doesn't matter how hard, wide, big you feel the dream is, with God all things are possible.

While in the process of waiting for God's intervention, if things get worse, that is not your problem but His.

In John 11, a family Jesus loved greatly invited Him to intervene in a case. They told Him, *Lazarus whom thou loveth is ill, come and heal him.* By the time He got there, the man was dead. You would have thought that since the problem got worse by the time He got there, He would apologize, but He knew all things are possible. Lazarus' sister Martha said, *Jesus, had you come earlier he wouldn't have died*, Jesus said *Do you know who is talking to you; I am the resurrection, I am the life.* She did not know that with and through Him all things are possible. Jesus carries the answer to all problems of life. She said *by now he has been dead for four days and he's probably stinking*. From their description no "good" could result from the matter, but when the Master showed up on the scene He showed them that with God all things are possible.

His power of possibility is not limited and doesn't expire. His name is "one size fits all problems." It doesn't matter what it is or the condition of it. It doesn't matter what man says, not even what the pastor says, for with God all things are possible.

This year my God will visit you and your family in the name of Jesus Christ.

When the Lord visited Abraham and his family, they received him well. He said to Abraham "Where is your wife?" he answered "She is in the tent making sure everything is well". He said, "By the time I return you will have a son." Sarah overheard and laughed looking at her condition. She had forgotten who was talking; she had forgotten it was God Almighty talking.

They didn't understand that the One talking to them is the Creator of the Heaven and Earth; He is the Manufacturer. Can a manufacturer who made something not be able to fix it?

The maker of her body (Sarah) changed everything that appeared to be bad, so she gave birth to the promise God had for her.

In this year 2015, especially this month of December you will birth your own promise in the name of Jesus Christ.

He told them *I am the LORD, the God of all flesh: is there anything too hard for me* (Jeremiah 32:27).

If you understand this matter you will live triumphantly; knowing your God is able to do above all you can ask or think. It doesn't matter what others, immigration, teachers, doctors have said, just know with God ALL things are possible.

And God returned back according to Genesis 21:1, *And the LORD visited Sarah as he had said, and the LORD did unto Sarah as he had spoken.*

I wish you know and understand the God you serve; that with and for Him all things are possible. There is no height He cannot lift you too, there is no prosperity He cannot give you, and there is no protection, increase, enlargement, promotion, and amount of peace He cannot give you. With your God, all things are possible. Time can't stop Him; length of years, day or night can't stop Him. They may roll stones on your way but that can't stop Him, the law of the land, your accent can't stop Him, NOTHING can stop Him.

Lift your voice and PRAISE HIM!

We want to thank Him for His ability and involvement in your 2015.

My Father, for agreeing to be part of my life in 2015, I am here to say thank you. For the things you are going to involve yourself in for me, my family and your church I am here to say thank you.

Beloved, now are we the sons of God, and it doth not yet appear what we shall be: but we know that, when He shall appear, we shall be like him; for we shall see him as He is (1 John 3:2).

Father, for what I, my family and your church are still going to be this year, especially this month of December, I am here to thank you in Jesus name.

Who you are determines what you are going to have. Our current president for example, his name or ancestry has not changed from what it was 20 years ago, but 20 years ago the Secret Service was not following him around; they are today, because of what he has become. What you become determines what you have.

What you are going to be, you have never seen before.

It means a new you is emerging. 1 Corinthians 2:9 says, *But as it is written, Eye hath not seen, nor ear heard, neither have entered into the heart of man, the things which God hath prepared for them that love him.*

Father, for the things I have not seen or become before, that my family and your church have not become, I am here to say thank you Lord.

December is the last month of 2015. If mercy brought you through November 2015, you will need mercy to see you through December 2015.

Father, throughout the month of December and the entire 2015 let your goodness and mercy follow me, my family and your church in the name of Jesus Christ.

So the Lord blessed the latter end of Job more than his beginning: for he had fourteen thousand sheep, and six thousand camels, and a thousand yoke of oxen, and a thousand she asses (Job 42:12)

Father, the month of December is the last month of 2015; let everything in December 2015

be better for me than the rest of the year combined in the name of Jesus.

I am as a wonder unto many; but thou art my strong refuge (Psalm 71:7). God will make you a wonder to your generation in the name of Jesus Christ.

Father, this year especially this month of December make me, my family and your church a wonder to many, a wonder to our generation in the name of Jesus.

Therefore, behold, I will proceed to do a marvelous work among this people, even a marvelous work and a wonder: for the wisdom of their wise men shall perish, and the understanding of their prudent men shall be hid (Isaiah 29:14).

Father, in me, within my family and your church you are going to do marvelous works and wonder this year in Jesus mighty name.

All through the year 2015, the Lord will protect your soul and life in this land of the living in the name of Jesus.

Wilt thou shew wonders to the dead? Shall the dead arise and praise thee (Psalm 88:10).

Father, throughout the year 2015 preserve my soul, my family, and your church and we will daily see your wonders in the name of Jesus.

He that dwelleth in the secret place of the most High shall abide under the shadow of the Almighty (Psalm 91:1).

Throughout the entire 2015, Father, keep me, my family, my loved ones, and your church. No evil will come our way in the name of Jesus.

Pray in the Holy Ghost

<u>My Prayer for You This Month:</u>

Oh Lord our Father we thank you again and again for these prayers. What an awesome God you are, what a glorious King you are, what a marvelous God you are and without any doubt you have done marvelous things. From the first day of this year to this day we are here to give you thanks and praises that is due to your name, we are grateful. Father, we don't have enough capacity to truly give you the thanks you deserve; you are worth a lot more than all our thanks. Take all the praise in the name of Jesus Christ. For the wonders in 2015 take all the praise. We cover ourselves in your blood for the remaining days in the year 2015. No evil will be heard of our story, our family and your church. For all the prayers all believers all over the world have prayed give us answers so that the world will know that we serve the God that answers prayers in Jesus precious name.

We dedicate the month of December 2015 to you in the name of the Father, Son and Holy Spirit.

Shout a tremendous Hallelujah!

Prayer Charge For December

I want to thank God for you and congratulate you because what will happen in your life in the remaining days of the year will amaze you in the name of Jesus Christ.

You need a prophet to guide you into your next season. God does not change seasons for His people without the guidance of the ministry of the prophet. So the things I am saying to you are the things God is saying to you, which you must embrace wholeheartedly.

Israel was going to change seasons; Jehoshaphat the captain of the tribe of Judah said, *believe in the Lord your God so thou shall be established. Believe his prophet so your journey may be prosperous.* Because of the ministry that God has given to us your journey throughout the remaining days of 2015 will be a prosperous one in the name of Jesus Christ.

Understanding the way the Bible works will make life work for you. If you don't know the way the Bible works, life will not work for you. It may seem it is working until challenges appear. I always tell people you don't need an umbrella if it is not raining. You may say you don't need a covering, this is true, as long as it is not raining. He said by prophet they came out of Egypt, by prophet they were preserved in the Promised Land.

A prophet is an ordinary man if he does not have God's word. So the value of the prophet is not the man himself, it is what he is telling you from God. Given this, I am telling you from God that your journey in throughout 2015 will be prosperous in the name of Jesus Christ.

You don't need to be in sin to suffer, righteous people suffer. *Many are the afflictions of the righteous.* Don't let the devil tell you, you are suffering because you are in sin. A righteous man can suffer, the Bible says *The righteous perish, and no one takes it to heart; the devout are taken away, and no one understands that the righteous are taken away to be spared from evil* (Isaiah 57:1)

When Pharaoh saw Jacob, he asked how old he was. Jacob responded one hundred and thirty years (Genesis 47:7-9), but Pharaoh countered that he looked older than his age. Jacob replied and said it was not he but the troubles of life. Any one using this devotional that life has aged, you are entering your youthful years in this month of December 2015 in the name of Jesus Christ. You will be looking younger, fresher than your age in the name of Jesus Christ. You will be looking nicer than your age in the name of Jesus Christ. You will be looking too good for your age in the name of Jesus Christ.

Pray: **Father, thank you for this new season coming my way, coming the way of my family, coming the way of your church, coming the way of our nation in the name of Jesus.**

How do I re-write my story? There are stories that become history and the world says history cannot be erased. It is true to an extent until you get God involved. 2 Corinthians 5:17 says *If any man be in Christ he is a new creature, old things have passed away, behold ALL things have become new.*

If your story is not rewritten it means life plays its music for you as usual. But when your story is rewritten you have a chance to dance to a new music.

In the remaining days of 2015, God is giving you another opportunity to dance to a new music in the name of Jesus Christ.

The scripture says he has blotted out every handwriting that was written against us. So history can be rewritten. Some histories are good; some are not good because they are against you. Colossians 2:14, *blotting out the handwriting of ordinance that was written against us which was contrary*, meaning that there are some things that won't work for your advantage, they would work for your adversity. Whatever is not going to work for your advantage in life will seize to operate in the name of Jesus Christ. Whatever is spoken against your destiny, whether you are aware of it or not God will rewrite that story in the name of Jesus Christ. *And He took it out of the way, nailing it to the cross and having spoiled principalities and powers, He made a shew of them openly, triumphing over them in it.* Your enemies will receive open shame in the name of Jesus Christ. (Colossians 2:14b-15)

In Genesis 49, we find the story of Jacob who also operated in the ministry of a prophet because he was telling his children how their lives will look in the future. Every father wants a bright future for his children but for Jacob, he brought the record of their worst offences to the One that would determine what their future would look like. Some of us have sown evil seeds in the past that is now affecting our future.

Genesis 49:1-2 says, *And Jacob called unto his sons and said gather yourselves together that I may tell you that which shall befall you in the last days. That the future ahead of you, I will tell you what is going to happen to you. Gather yourselves together, and hear, ye sons of Jacob; and hearken unto Israel your father.* He didn't speak to them in his old nature, he invoked his covenant right over their lives as Israel. This man meant business. Jacob called them but Israel spoke to them.

Jacob did this because he was placing whatever he was saying upon the covenant that God made with him when he changed his name to Israel. Genesis 49:3 says, *Reuben, thou art my firstborn, my might, and the beginning of my strength, the excellency of dignity, and the excellency of power.* Anyone would have been excited at that opening statement, but all of a sudden the tone changed. Genesis 49:4a, *Unstable as water, thou shalt not excel.*

Reuben should naturally have had a bright future but words of man put him under limitation. That is why I want to beg parents, our children will provoke us, our children will mistreat us, lets be careful what we say. Do your best at your highest annoyance to just keep quiet because what you say may need divine intervention to reverse it.

Jacob didn't say much to Reuben. He pretty much said though you are supposed to be this, I place upon you the curse of instability, nothing will work again for you, nothing will last in your hands, everything will crumble and miss their journey. He placed a mandate on his maximum - you will not excel. Meaning whatever Reuben was doing he could never excel at it or enjoy maximum. This was because *thou wentest up to thy father's bed; then defiledst thou it: he went up to my couch.* The question is when Reuben did what he did Jacob never said anything. He kept quiet (Genesis 35: 21-22). He waited for when his life should have been be bright, then the devil entered and put things in his mouth to say against his first son.

Genesis 49:5-6, *Simeon and Levi are brethren; instruments of cruelty are in their habitations. O my soul, come not thou into their secret; unto their assembly, mine honour, be not thou united: for in their anger they slew a man, and in their selfwill they digged down a wall.* Levi was supposed to be the priesthood of the Lord. The people that are not permitted to labor by the design of God but here Jacob is exempting them from every provision God has made for them. He didn't stop there, he said *my honor be not united unto them for in their anger they slew a man, and in their selfwill they digged down a wall.* Genesis 49:7, *Cursed be their anger, for it was fierce; and their wrath, for it was cruel: I will divide them in Jacob, and scatter them in Israel.* See the quantity of curses he placed on his first three children.

Genesis 49:8, *Judah, thou art he whom thy brethren shall praise.* The Lord had to step in because Judah means Praise and since He was coming to the earth to save mankind, He would need a family. God inhabits the praises of His people and this automatically made Judah His family. Given this, He had to stop the progression of the curse because His family cannot be cursed. Remember, Jesus Christ is called the Lion of the tribe of Judah (Revelation 5:5) otherwise, he would have kept cursing all those children because he was venting over what they had done to him. He was still going to come to the issue of Joseph. Don't forget, the next person whom he would have cursed was Judah, because he was the one that counseled his brethren to sell Joseph the son he loved, the son of his old age.

Reuben was the one that said don't kill him but Judah was the one that said sell him. Don't forget he was bringing their history and placing judgment on their future. Everything Reuben did, he was cursed for it. Everything Simeon and Levi did, they got cursed for it. So he was going to take all what Judah had done to place the curse on him but God said, I need a family when I am coming, I am using this one to stop the curse. When Jesus is involved in your life He can stop a curse before it reaches you. That is why I want to tell you that going forward, embrace Him so He can get more involved in your life and affairs too by His grace. If not what affects others will affect you.

Do you know the good news? Since He stepped in for Judah there was no curse any longer. The curse only stayed with Reuben, Simeon and Levi. So Judah became the history rewriter just like as Jesus Christ who stopped curses by hanging on the cross (Galatians 3:13). There is somebody using this prayer devotional that will become the Judah of his or her family. A Judah of their generation. A Judah of their country. A Judah of the world.

Say, **Father, make me the Judah of my generation. Father, make me the Judah of my family. Father, make me the Judah of this nation.**

It is important to understand that Jesus is our curse breaker. Some things are called windbreakers and are planted to break the wind in areas that are prone to high winds. Jesus is your curse breaker; He broke the curse because Judah in future was going to house Him.

Allow Jesus to be in your heart, let Him rule your home, let Him rule your business. You will continue in chaos if you don't let Him take His place. For three months, Obededom allowed the ark to stay in his house; three months their story changed for the better. Embrace the Lord like never before. If you will serve Him, He said He will bless your bread and water and remove sicknesses far from you.

Serving God is what preserved my health. The moment I stop serving God, I might begin to fall ill like others. I saw the scripture that this is the way to be healthy, and signed up for it. 1992 was the last time I took medication I have not tasted medication since. Sometime ago, I went for my physical and my primary care physician said I had high blood pressure. He said he would place me on medication. I said no, give me one week to come back and then you will check it again. I went to God; and said God, I saw something I have never seen before, high blood pressure, I hear about it and also pray against it. God said do you know why it is there? I said No. God said you are too worried for what you are not supposed to be worrying about. This occurred in 2010, when our church was moving from one location to another. I put upon myself the burden that was not my burden. I went back to God and said "God I'm sorry, you are the One that bears burdens. Carry it". The following week, I returned to my physician, had my blood pressure checked, and to his surprise, it was normal. And of course, he wondered what I did.

If they serve me I will bless their bread and water and remove sickness.

The question is; does the story above (diatribe) mean it was over for Reuben, Simeon and Levi? No. Let's take a look at how the Master corrected it. Deuteronomy 33:1-3, *And this is the blessing, wherewith Moses the man of God blessed the children of Israel before his death. And he said, The LORD came from Sinai, and rose up from Seir unto them; he shined forth from mount Paran, and he came with ten thousands of saints: from his right hand went a fiery law for them. Yea, he loved the people; all his saints are in thy hand: and they sat down at thy feet; every one shall receive of thy words.*

One way to connect eternally with blessings is to sit where the word of God is. Sit where you hear the word of God, don't roam around. Your life is secured anywhere the word of God is. Sit down there. They sat in the place of His word.

Deuteronomy 33:4-6, *Moses commanded us a law, even the inheritance of the congregation of Jacob. And he was king in Jeshurun, when the heads of the people and the tribes of Israel were gathered together. Let Reuben live, and not die; and let not his men be few.* Just as Jacob gathered them, Moses did likewise. Don't forget Jacob his father had said he will not excel but what did Moses say? *And let not his men be few* meaning let him multiply, let him increase, let him enlarge, let him enjoy maximum. What the father had said, Moses countered it.

Jacob wrote the first story from the mouth of Israel but the second story was written by Moses with God. So God decided to remove the curse on Reuben. I come as your Moses now to take you from where you are to where you ought to be.

Pray this prayer violently. You are going to cover yourself in the blood of Jesus from your foundation.

Lord, from my foundation to where I am and to where I am going, I cover everything in your precious blood.

Father, I am here now for a new history, for a new story, for a new season, cover my destiny, cover my life, cover my family, cover your church with your blood from our foundation to where we are and to where we are going. Cover us in your blood.

Father, I have signaled to Heaven, beginning from now give me a new story in the name of Jesus.

Father, we don't deserve a new story; we do not qualify for a new story. We are not making our demands based on what we deserve, we are not making our demands based on what we qualify for. We are making our demands on your sacrifice. We have seen what you sacrificed and we know we can place a demand on the sacrifice. Upon your sacrifice we place a demand for a new story, beginning from now in the name of Jesus Christ. Take all the glory Father in Jesus name we pray.

Lord, we release your people now, there's no doubt that all the blessings of the Year of Maximum will be made manifest in their lives. We therefore announce to the year of maximum, hear the word of God and secure their place for them in the name of Jesus Christ. Make all things well for them in the name of Jesus Christ. Let their joy be full. We dedicate 2015 to you Father, in the name of the Father, the Son and the Holy Spirit. Thank you heavenly Father, in Jesus name we pray.

Whatever that represents your future in your hands are blessed in the name of Jesus. Congratulations.

Epilogue

Every time God answers the prayers of His people, and/or every time He makes a promise for an intervention, He expects praise to return to Him. He is very jealous for His praise. He expects it and He is worthy of it. Psalm 29:2 says, *Give unto the LORD the glory due unto his name; worship the LORD in the beauty of holiness.*

Luke 17:11-17, tells the story of the ten lepers, who were healed by Jesus. As He healed them, the ten lepers went on their way, to where Jesus asked them to go. Suddenly they discovered that they had been healed of their infirmity; ten came and ten got the healing. This means He always makes sure no one is left behind. In the blessing of 2015, you will not be left behind in the name of Jesus Christ. Whatever you requested from Him, you will find it in your life and destiny; you will discover that it has been added to you in the name of Jesus Christ.

You have come to Him and you will get your desired miracle in the name of Jesus. Nobody comes to Him, and goes empty handed. Isaiah 45:19b says *I said not unto the seed of Jacob, Seek ye me in vain: I the LORD speak righteousness, I declare things that are right.*

When the ten discovered they had been healed, one returned to thank Him. Only one returned to give a testimony and to sing a special song.

Jesus said, were there not ten that was cleansed, and where are the other nine? Why is it only one that returned? Why are people very ungrateful after God has visited them, after they have received healing, deliverance, and/or intervention from Him?

You don't have to see your miracle, before you believe He has done it. Numbers 23:19 says, *God is not a man, that he should lie; neither the son of man, that he should repent: hath he said, and shall he not do it? or hath he spoken, and shall he not make it good?*

It's important to always return to give glory to Him. Don't wait until you see it. Return and give glory to Him, and see if He will not do it. When you give Him praise for a miracle that He has not done, you commit Him to doing it. If He doesn't do it, He will have to return your praise to you, and the Bible says in Isaiah 42:8, *I am the LORD: that is my name: and my glory will I not give to another...* So, commit Him, by giving praise before you see the miracle. Once you commit Him by your praise, there is no way you will not rejoice after.

Luke 17:15-16 says, *And one of them, when he saw that he was healed, turned back, with a loud voice glorifying God; and he fell upon his face at his feet, giving him thanks: and he was a Samaritan.* There is always one more miracle for those who return. The other nine thought they had been healed, if they knew they needed to me made whole, after receiving their healing they would have returned. It's as if the master, deliberately withholds a miracle. The extra miracle remaining for 2015, you are getting it now in Jesus name.

The reason you will get it, is because you have returned to give thanks. As the man returned, he got the extra. Anytime you return and give a testimony, you receive your one more miracle.

The leper that returned didn't know there was one more miracle, he just returned to give thanks. Thank God you now know that anytime you return to give thanks, there is one more miracle waiting for you. The advantage you have is that you know, because the scripture has recorded it for your benefit.

Father, I have returned to give glory, honor and adoration to you for myself, my family, all my loved ones and your church. I have returned to you who enabled me to pray. For giving me the privilege to be part of the living, and to participate in these Prayers for my 2015, I thank you.

You want to thank Him for all the promises He made to you during these prayers. God made a lot of promises to us during these prayers.

Father, for all the promises made to me concerning January, February, March, April, May, June, July, August, September, October, November, December 2015 I am here to say thank you.

Father, for all you are going to make me in the year 2015, for the way my life is going to look in this 2015, for what I will become in this 2015; I am here to give thanks for myself, my family and your church.

Thank Him for the extra that He will give you. Bible says in Ephesians 3:20 *Now unto him that is able to do exceeding abundantly above all that we ask or think, according to the power that worketh in us*, which means that beyond the things that you have asked He is able to do exceeding abundantly about it.

Father, for all the extras waiting for me, my family and your church in this 2015, I am here to thank you.

Father, we have thanked you over everything we can thank you for. We know that our thanksgiving will never be enough, because you have done too much for us, but for the thanksgiving we have brought, please accept it in the name of Jesus Christ.

We dedicate the entire 2015 to you in the name of the Father, the Son and of the Holy Sprit, in Jesus precious name we worship.

Have a Blessed Day

Other books by Emmanuel Olowokere

Praise My Key To A High Place is a review of the revelation of the glory of God through praise and the manifestation of the role of praise and the reward for praise of the Almighty.

Prayer Weapons for 2014 is a collection of prayers that enables you sow the greatest seed you can sow for your future, the seed of prayer. It's a weapon in your hands to fight for your future. If you can fight for your future, you can possess it and this tool will assist you in guaranteeing a successful future. These prayer topics are as relevant to you today as they were in 2014.